new home furniture design
muebles de diseño
últimas tendencias

NEW HOME FURNITURE DESIGN
MUEBLES DE DISEÑO últimas tendencias
Copyright ©2007 Instituto Monsa de ediciones

Editor
Josep María Minguet

Art Director
Louis Bou

Layout
Maquetación
Eva Minguet Cámara

Translation
Traducción
Babyl Traducciones

©INSTITUTO MONSA DE EDICIONES
Gravina 43 (08930)
Sant Adrià de Besòs
Barcelona
Tlf. +34 93 381 00 50
Fax.+34 93 381 00 93
www.monsa.com
monsa@monsa.com

ISBN 10 84-96429-39-3
ISBN 13 978-84-96429-39-0
D.L B-5.136-2.007

Printed by
Indústrias Gráficas Mármol

new home furniture design

muebles de diseño

últimas tendencias

contents

Cooking with design!
¡Cocinar con estilo!
10 - 41

Living cool!
Salones de ensueño
42 - 95

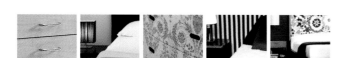

Bedtime stories
Descansa con diseño
96 - 125

Play, fun and sweet dreams!
¡Juega, diviértete y dulces sueños!
126 - 153

Free time for everybody
Tiempo libre para todos
154 - 181

Working at home
Trabajando en casa
182 - 206

Please, do not disturb
Porfavor, no molestar
206 - 231

In my secret garden
Mi jardín secreto
232 - 255

contenido

intro

Human being is characterized, amongst other things, by our fondness not only for other beings but also for the elements around us which form a part of our daily lives and to which we attach a sentimental value. These elements appear largely in our homes, our one and only refuge, the place we turn for rest and relaxation, where we seek warmth and comfort and where our lives are reflected in the furniture and objects we have acquired at different times and under different circumstances.

In this book we make a virtual tour of the home, from the living room to the kitchen, from the children's bedroom to outside, recreating each and every one of these spaces with the aid of a very careful selection taken both from the manufacturers and designers of the world's latest creations. This could actually be said to be a tour of many homes, filled with ideas which, like a puzzle, are broken into thousands of tiny pieces liable to tally with any number of very diverse forms.

It has to be said that furniture design needs to continuously come up with ideas which are appropriate to the needs of modern day lifestyles: the new home concept, which in some cases includes the place of work, the varied uses of the furniture itself, the scarcity of work space and lack of resources and finally the appearance of new materials which add a new dimension to the pieces of furniture produced. The result is a combination of the modern and the traditional, today's top furniture designers having looked back as a means of bringing forth some incredibly creative results.

El ser humano se caracteriza entre otras muchas cosas por su apego no sólo a otros seres sino también a otros elementos que le rodean y forman parte de su vida, cargándolos de una aureola sentimental. Es en la casa donde estos elementos aparecen en mayor número, por ser nuestro refugio y lugar de descanso, donde buscamos la calidez y comodidad, y por ser un reflejo de nuestra vida con la diversidad de elementos y muebles adquiridos en momentos y circunstancias diferentes.

En este libro realizamos un paseo virtual por la casa, pasando desde la sala de estar a la cocina, desde la habitación infantil al espacio exterior, recreando todos estos espacios con las últimas creaciones realizadas en el mundo, con una cuidadosa selección tanto de los fabricantes como de los diseñadores. Es más, diríamos que es un paseo por muchas casas, muchas propuestas que como un rompecabezas, se fragmentan en miles de piezas susceptibles de encajar de formas muy diversas.

Es importante señalar que el diseño de mobiliario va planteando fórmulas adecuadas a las nuevas necesidades vitales: un nuevo concepto de casa, que incluye a veces el espacio de trabajo, la diversidad en la funcionalidad de los muebles, la escasez de espacio y de recursos y la aparición de nuevos materiales añadiendo una nueva dimensión a las piezas que se fabrican. Se logra por tanto una mezcla entre tradición y modernidad donde los grandes diseñadores del mueble actual miran al pasado para lograr como se verá unos resultados tremendamente fértiles.

The kitchen concept has been continuously evolving from the very earliest of times until it has finally become one of the most important and sophisticated rooms in the house.
From the gas rings, invented more than a hundred years ago, to the present day concept, which almost likens the kitchen to a laboratory, a long process has taken place which is not entirely unrelated to the changes in society itself. The kitchen is a welcoming place, a base for family life, for quick snacks and informal meals or even the place to hold a get together with the closest of friends.
The following pages reveal a wide range of the latest designs for modern kitchens which also meet the needs of a modern society.

Desde los tiempos más primitivos el concepto de cocina ha ido evolucionando hasta llegar a convertirse en una de las piezas más importantes y sofisticadas de la casa.
Desde el hornillo de gas inventado hace más de cien años hasta la concepción actual, que convierte la cocina en un auténtico laboratorio, hay un largo proceso que no es ajeno a los cambios de la sociedad. La cocina es un lugar agradable, arta para la vida familiar, para las comidas rápidas e informales o, incluso, para la tertulia con los amigos más allegados.
En las páginas que siguen, se presenta un amplio exponente de los últimos diseños en complementos para la creación de espacios en las cocinas modernas que cumplan con las necesidades de la sociedad actual.

AMICA
Designed by Leicht
Made by LEICHT
www.leicht.de

The kitchen needs new colours! in particular the new elegant Bordeaux shade for the AMICA model, a high gloss laminate front, is a favourite. The Diagonal-Centre as a projecting, preparation area, accessible from three sides, invites "communicative" kitchen work. Apart from red, AMICA is available in ice blue, vanilla, frosty white, platinum, anthracite and in the new striking wood décor macassar which provides highlights in single coloured kitchens. The AMICA-fronts are faced in melamine resin laminate, the front being high gloss, the reverse matt textured.

¡La cocina necesita nuevos colores! El modelo AMICA lleva especialmente una novedosa tonalidad , con lo que su puerta estratificada de alto brillo aparece como muy grande. El elemento puente, como una zona de preparación, colocada hacia delante y asequible por tres de sus lados, posibilita un trabajo de cocina "comunicativo". Además de en rojo, el modelo AMICA existe en las tonalidades azul polar, vainilla, blanco nieve, platino, antracita y en la nueva y remarcable decoración makassar, con lo cual se consigue marcar acentos, sobre todo en las cocinas monocolor.

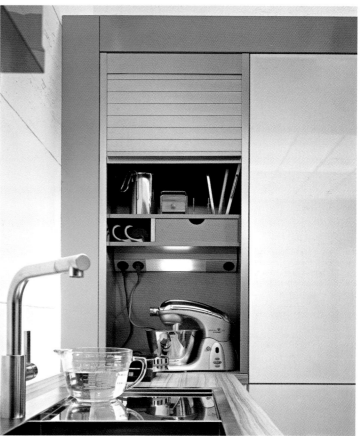

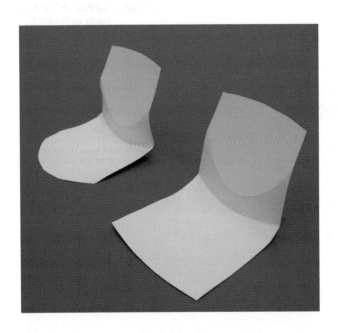

Folding Lines

FOLDING PLYWOOD LIKE ORIGAMI

Bend

Fold Up

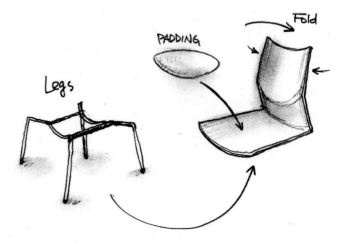

PADDING

Fold

Legs

KAI Chair
Designed by Shin Azumi
Made by LAPALMA
www.azumi.co.uk
www.lapalma.it

Playing with paper, was the start of this project. If you fold a piece of paper you get a crisp edge, and if you bend it you get a gentle but tensioned curvature. I tried to fix the beauty of these natural phenomena as a chair. The name, KAI, is a Japanese word. Its pronunciation can be interpreted in several different ways. KAI can be a seashell. The oppositional two elliptical lines recall an opened seashell. KAI can be comfort. KAI can be meeting. KAI can be answer. KAI can be pioneer...

Este proyecto se crea a partir de jugar con papel. Si doblamos un trozo de papel obtenemos un borde afilado, y si por otro lado lo curvamos conseguimos una curva suave pero tensa. Shin Azumi creó esta silla inspirado por la belleza de estos fenómenos naturales. El nombre "KAI" es una palabra japonesa que tiene distintos significados, puede ser una concha marina, de hecho las líneas de la silla nos recuerdan a una concha. KAI puede ser comfort. KAI puede ser un encuentro. KAI puede ser ...

FLAP TABLE
Designed by Karim Rashid
Made by BONALDO
www.karimrashid.com
www.bonaldo.com

Small and large, closed and opened: FLAP is modern and original both in its structure and its colors. The table top in rigid polyurethane has a scratch-proof varnish and rests on a central base of chrome-plated steel. Two wing-type extensions "lift" symmetrically creating room to comfortably seat six people. The colors, proposed in two original combinations – white top with silver extensions or green top with pink extensions – make the table more precious and lively. FLAP combines practicality and romanticism and it is perfect for the more creative kitchens and dining rooms.

Grande y pequeño, cerrado y abierto: FLAP es moderna y original tanto en sus colores como en su estructura. La tabla de la mesa está fabricada en poliuretano barnizado a prueba de arañazos y descansa en una base central de acero cromado. Dos alas extensibles se elevan simétricamente para dar espacio cómodamente a seis personas. Los dos colores propuestos son: mesa blanca con alas plateadas o mesa verde con las alas de color rosado. FLAP combina practicidad y romanticismo y es perfecta para las cocinas o comedores más creativos.

AMICA
Designed by Leicht
Made by LEICHT
www.leicht.it

In the glossy white AMICA with its characteristic dark edge contouring, a generous wooden table marks the transition to the living area. Wall and floor units here are extra wide, providing a visually diagonal and an open calm room effect. The wall bound kitchen furniture are framed and emphasised by side panels with integrated lighting. The material of the made-to-measure worktops with vertical panels, is stainless steel; the elegant niche wall in the sink area is created from black acrylic.

Una amplia mesa de madera señala el paso a la zona habitable de la casa sobre el blanco brillante del modelo AMICA, con sus característicos filos oscuros, que lo enmarcan. Los muebles altos y bajos se han dispuesto aquí con sobreancho. Con ello se alcanza una impresión óptica orientada en dirección horizontal y un ambiente, abierto y apacible, del espacio. Los muebles de cocina colocados sobre la pared quedan enmarcados y acentuados por paneles, con iluminación integrada. El material de las encimeras, acabadas en serie, con paneles verticales, es el acero inoxidable.

CINQUETERRE
Designed by Vico Magistretti
Made by SCHIFFINI
www.schiffini.it

Aluminium is the structural element of the doors, which have a wave-shaped profile and organically integrate with fine handles made of aluminium or wood. Equipped peninsular units and large hoods are all distinctive elements permitting infinite kitchen solutions in which design, refinement and high quality materials collectively make up the common denominator. Doors are in anodized aluminium. The linearity of design, the preciosity of materials, the compositions with sliding glass doors which can be incorporated in wall, base and peninsular-island units make the CINQUETERRE a unique kitchen, not only the first kitchen to be entirely realized in aluminium, but also a refined and personalized product.

Las puertas de aluminio sobresalen por su elegancia y por los resultados extraordinarios, que se apuntan en el rubro de la duración, de la higiene y de la elevada precisión de los procesos constructivos que les dieron vida. La puerta de perfil ondulado se realiza mediante láminas de aluminio anodizado natural superpuestas. El respaldo y el fondo de los muebles son de laminado HPL blanco, de 4 mm de espesor, resistente al agua. Madera impermeable, se construye mediante madera regenerada 100% (panel ecológico), de 18 mm de espesor, chapada en melamina.

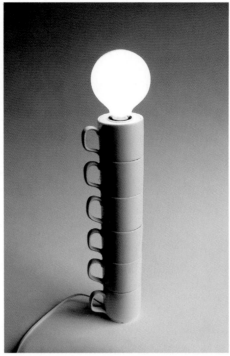
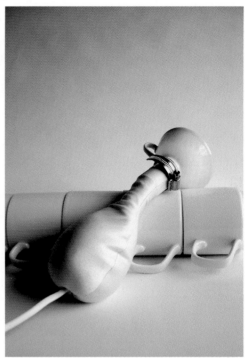

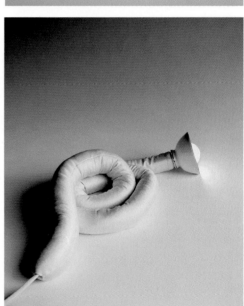

THE CUP LAMP
Designed by Malin Lundmark
Made by MALIN LUNDMARK
www.malinlundmark.com

Designer Malin Lundmark has designed a collection of amazing lamps made from old coffe cups and plates. Each lamp is one of a kind so we can find them hanging on the wall in its own ear, a table lamp where different plates stacked on each other creates a lamp foot, a table lamp which has a flexible body and a coffe cup as lamp shade, three tea cups stacked on each other creating a pendant lamp, a flexible lamp in the shape of a snake...
The combinations are infinite!

La diseñadora Malin Lundmark ha creado una fantástica y exclusiva colección de lámparas hechas con tazas y platos de café antiguos. Cada lámpara es única y podemos encontrarlas colgadas en la pared por su propio asa, o en una lámpara de mesa en la que diferentes platitos amontonados forman el pié, otra lámpara de cuerpo flexible en el que una taza hace de pantalla, en forma de serpiente...
¡Las combinaciones son infinitas!

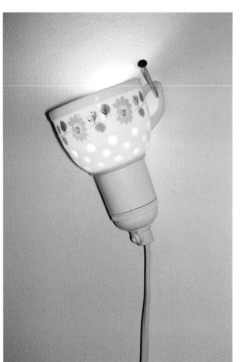

MODUS
Designed by Paolo Nava & Fabio Casiraghi
Made by BINOVA
www.binova.com

MODUS re-formulates the relationship between the kitchen and living room, re-defining these areas as a "living kitchen". The series re-works the typical meaning of the kitchen and living room as environments, transforming itself into architecture by becoming a representative symbol or an elegant and essential laboratory. Therefore, the curtains have been conceived to turn the architecture of the kitchen and home into an architectural element that changes the perspective of space and focuses one's attention on the worktops.
The materials used in the MODUS system have been selected to maintain its relationship with the ideals of wealth: the essence and expressive nature of wood, stone and steel.

MODUS se enfrenta con la relación de interacción entre cocina y sala de estar, la cocina-living, en el uso de un lenguaje capaz de coordinar cocina y sala de estar en la típica acepción de ambiente, para transformarse en arquitectura que se viste con   símbolos de representación o como elegante y sintético laboratorio. De aquí el uso de los bastidores, concebidos para transformar la arquitectura de la cocina y de la casa, como un elemento arquitectónico que puede modificar la prospectiva del espacio, capaces de concentrar la atención sobre las encimeras.
Los materiales de MODUS mantienen una relación con ideales de prestigio: la materialidad y la carga expresiva de la madera, como las de la piedra y el acero, disimulan los tecnicismos en favor del ambiente.

G.BOX
Designed by Giuliano Giaroli
Made by SCHIFFINI
www.schiffini.it

Carbon fibre bonded with white Carrara marble and bamboo is combined with tempered glass for the doors and a cellular aluminium alloy for the worktops. The worktop extends sideways and down to the floor, covering the short side of the island made up of thick glass (15mm), white Carrara marble with cellular aluminium alloy and bamboo veneer. These metallic elements can either house cooking hobs or serve as a breakfast bar.

Al vidrio templado se añaden el bambú y el mármol blanco de Carrara unido a fibra de carbono para la puerta, y con alveolar de aluminio para la encimera. La encimera de trabajo continúa lateralmente hasta el suelo, recubriendo el lado corto de la isla y está previsto en un vidrio de gran espesor (15 mm), en mármol blanco de Carrara confeccionado con alveolar de aluminio, y en multicapa de bambú. Estos elementos en acero pueden ser usados como contenedores de encimeras de cocción de encastre, o como bancos de desayuno.

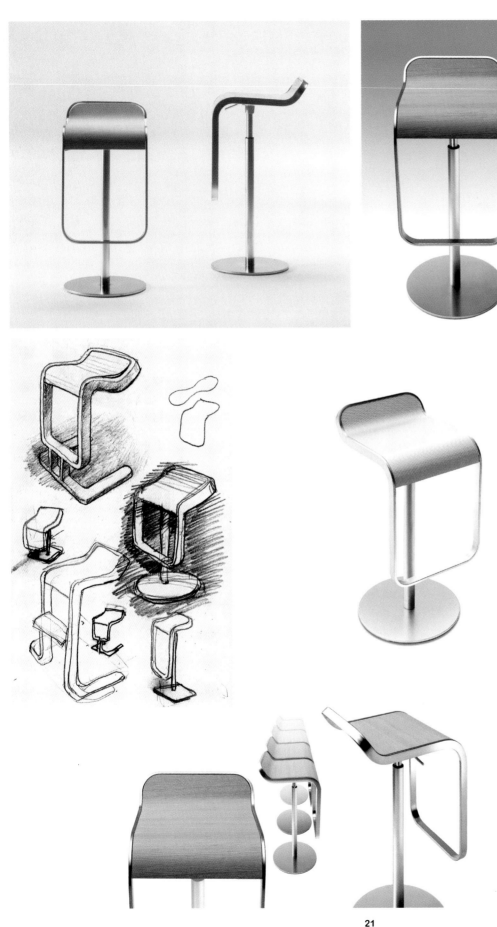

LEM STOOL
Designed by Shin & Tomoko Azumi
Made by LAPALMA
www.azumi.co.uk
www.lapalma.it

A high stool with swivel seat and gas spring height adjustable function. The seat and the foot rest are connected together and always provide a comfortable distance.
Seat: bleached Beech or dark Walnut veneered plywood, White and Black lacquered, Upholstered in leather/ fabric.
Structure and foot rest: Steel tube stain Chrome plated.
W=350 D=420 H=650 / 750 mm
FX International Design Award, UK.

Azumi nos presenta un taburete alto con altura ajustable gracias a su función de gas. El asiento y el reposa-pies están conectados proporcionando siempre una cómoda distancia.
Asiento: puede ser fabricado en haya blanqueada o nogal oscuro contrachapado, en color blanco y negro lacado o tapizado en cuero o tela.
Estructura y reposa pies: Tubo de acero cromado plateado.
W=350 D=420 H=650 / 750 mm
Ganador del premio FX International Design Award, UK.

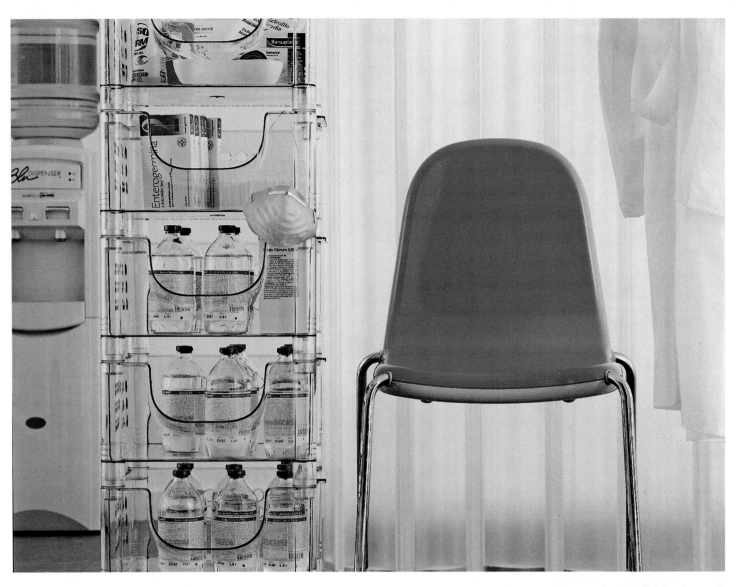

BUTTERFLY
Designed by Karim Rashid
Made by MAGIS
www.magisdesign.com
www.karimrashid.com

MAGIS brings us this appealing collection of ergonomically designed stacking chairs designed by Karim Rashid. Available in a range of flamboyant colours designed to add a cheerful touch to the kitchen. Materials: frame in polished steel tube. Seat and reverse of seat in standard injection-moulded polished ABS.

De la mano del diseñador Karim Rashid, MAGIS nos presenta esta divertida colección de sillas de diseño ergonómico que pueden apilarse fácilmente entre sí. Disponible en llamativos colores aportan un toque divertido a la cocina.
Materiales: marco en tubo de acero pulido. El asiento y reverso del asiento estan modelados por inyección ABS.

DOVE
Designed by A & H Van Onck
Made by MAGIS
www.magisdesign.com

These decorative and practical super sized stacking baskets are ideal for food storage and for keeping the kitchen tidy. Wheels can be added to the base, making it easy to move them from one place to another.

Cestas apilables super decorativas y muy prácticas para almacenar comida y tener en orden las cosas de la cocina. Podemos añadir unas ruedas en la estantería base para moverlas de un sitio a otro con total libertad.

TUTTIFRUTTI
Designed by Stefano Giovannoni
Made by MAGIS
www.magisdesign.com

Italian company MAGIS brings us these bright transparent methacrylate resin shelves designed by Stefano Giovannoni. Created in acid toned colours, these self-stacking shelves provide an excellent storage option for the kitchen.

De la mano de Stefano Giovannoni, la firma italiana MAGIS nos presenta estas llamativas estanterías de metacrilato transparente. Diseñadas en colores ácidos son apilables entre sí por lo que se convierten en un remedio estupendo para el almacenamiento en la cocina.

TRANSIT
Designed by David Mellor
Made by MAGIS
www.magisdesign.com

Tidiness in a small kitchen is essential. This shelf unit can be used either as an occasional kitchen table, somewhere to store fruit and vegetables or as a trolley to transport the meal from the kitchen to dining room. Once folded it takes up very little space and can be kept in any corner.

El orden en una cocina de tamaño reducido es esencial. Esta estantería puede ser utilizada a su vez como mesa auxiliar en la cocina, tanto para el almacenamiento de frutas y verduras, como para transportar la comida de la cocina al salón. Una vez plegada ocupa tan poco espacio que se puede guardar en cualquier rincón.

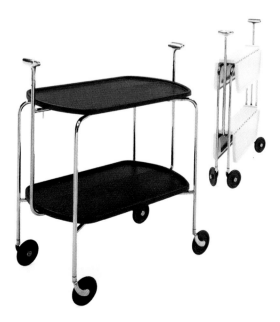

PLUSMODO
Designed by Jorge Pensi
Made by POGGEN POHL
www.poggenpohl.de

Open and closed: PLUSMODO is a powerful, poetic dialogue between presentation and concealment.
Poggenpohl and Jorge Pensi: One of the world's most prestigious kitchen brands and a much-acclaimed international designer demonstrate the fascination of a new idea of form. An aesthetic alliance proving that good design can never be anonymous.

Abierto y cerrado: PLUSMODO ofrece un diálogo vital y poético entre el exhibir y el ocultar.
Poggenpohl y Jorge Pensi: Una de las marcas de cocina de mayor prestigio del mundo y un diseñador internacional galardonado en múltiples ocasiones presentan la fascinación de un nuevo concepto de cocina. Una estética que demuestra que el buen diseño no puede ser anónimo.

SPEZIE
Designed by Ludovica y Roberto Palomba
Made by SCHIFFINI
www.schiffini.it

This exquisite kitchen design from SHIFFINI is the work of designers Ludovica and Roberto Palomba. The kitchen layout can be designed in accordance with the available space. The 4cm thick worktops are covered in a highly water resistant laminate as are the cabinets. The impermeable wood is made from a 100% recycled wood source in the form of 18mm thick eco-friendly - melamine veneer panels.

Un diseño exquisito para esta cocina de la firma SHIFFINI diseñada por Ludovica y Roberto Palomba. La cocina se puede configurar de distintas maneras según el espacio del que disponemos. La encimera, de cuatro centímetros de espesor, y el resto de la composición están laminados con un material altamente resistente al agua. La madera impermeable se construye a partir de madera regenerada 100% convertida en paneles ecológicos de 18 mm de espesor chapados en melamina.

DIAMETROTRENTACINQUE CUCINA INOX
Designed by Davide Vercelli
Made by RITMONIO
www.ritmonio.it

This amazing and original tap from the prestigious Italian company RITMONIO, has been made completely from stainless steel to completely eliminate any lead discharge caused by the water passing through. A notable feature is the flexible pull-out hose which proves to be particularly useful when it comes to washing the dishes.

La prestigiosa firma italiana RITMONIO nos presenta este fantástico y original grifo, fabricado completamente en acero inoxidable para eliminar por completo la liberación de plomo al paso del agua. Destaca la manguera extraíble también de acero inoxidable que nos da una libertad completa a la hora de fregar los platos.

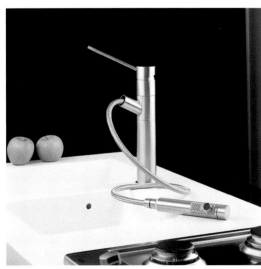

QUADRA
Designed by Arrital Cuine
Made by ARRITAL CUINE
www.arritalcuine.com

METHRA
Designed by Arrital
Made by ARRITAL CUINE
www.arritalcuine.com

METHRA's kitchen door is made by a panel lined with high quality PVC in several finishes: matt or glossy, the panel comes matt lacquered or glossy, adding also the colors plywood natural oak, dark oak and teak.
The top sheets in porphyry (natural stone) or monochromatic or in quartz.

La puerta de esta cocina METHRA está realizada por un panel forrado en PVC de alta calidad en varios acabados mate y brillo o el panel viene lacado al "agua" en los acabados mate , brillo y texturizado añadiendo también los colores contrachapado del roble natural, roble oscuro y teca.
Las encimeras se aconsejan en porfido (piedra natural) o en láminado Unicolor o en cuarzo.

The kitchen and lounge are combined in a single room, a symbol of the evolution of the "house" concept. Teak is the "leitmotiv" in which the solidity of the wood provides a contrast against the luminous "mirror" effect lacquered panes. QUADRA is characterized by genuine teak plywood doors with a choice of either teak or aluminium handles.

La cocina y la zona de estar se incorporan en un único espacio, símbolo de la evolución del concepto "casa" . La madera de teca es el "leitmotiv" donde la solidez de la madera se compara con la luminosidad de los cristales lacados , efecto "espejo". QUADRA se caracteriza por las puertas contrachapadas en verdadera madera de teca , el tirador esta' disponible sea en madera de teca o en aluminio.

BOX ONE SYSTEM & SPACE SYSTEM
Designed by Schiffini
Made by SCHIFFINI
www.schiffini.it

The Solaro kitchen explicitly affirms the relationship between SCHIFFINI and the sea. The walnut slats with black inlays characterise its design and are reminiscent of the teak roof of a boat, here taken onto a vertical surface, enriched by the semicircular metal handle. A blatantly glamorous kitchen, it combines the neatness of its design with the warmth of the materials of doors and top.

La cocina Solaro reafirma la relación entre la firma SCHIFFINI y el mar. Los listones de madera de nogal con hendidos de color negro caracterizan su diseño y nos recuerdan a la azotea de teca de un barco. Los tiradores metálicos semicirculares embellecen y ponen la guinda a esta cocina descaradamente glamurosa que combina la pulcritud de su diseño con el calor de los materiales de puertas y superficies.

INTEGRATION
Designed by Jorge Pensi
Made by POGGEN POHL
www.poggenpohl.de

A long and exciting journey. A journey that starts back in the early 1960s when Poggenpohl begins to develop the overriding kitchen idea. Commissioned design studies, such as the futuristic ball kitchen by Colani, see the daring integration of design, architecture technology and new media as a utopian vision. A dream has taken place. A home that welcomes you.

Un camino largo y excitante. Se inició a comienzos de los años 60, cuando Poggenpohl empezó a desarollar el concepto superior de cocina. Los audaces estudios de diseño realizados por encargo de Poggenpohl, como la cocina esférica futurista de Colani contempla la intégración de diseño, arquitectura, tecnología y nuevos medios como una visión utópica. El sueño se ha convertido en realidad. un hogar que le da a usted la bienvenida.

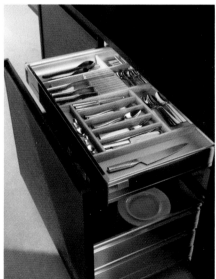

MODUS
Designed by Paolo Nava & Fabio Casiraghi
Made by BINOVA
www.binova.com

MODUS is the result of a quasi-preliminary path that can be read in many ways. It is a kitchen that opens up toward the living room, composed of furniture and architecture. The name "MODUS" has been chosen to tell the story of this project. It refers to the modus operandi, the method, and the interpretation that can be used in the kitchen area, or everything that revolves around it. MODUS is not a final destination but merely a stop on a journey that is completely new every day.

MODUS es el fruto de un recorrido, casi propedéutico, que puede ser interpretado de diversas maneras, una cocina abierta hacia el living, compuesta por muebles o por arquitectura. "MODUS" es el nombre elegido para narrar este proyecto, porque hace referencia al modus operandi, al método, a la interpretación que puede asumir el espacio de una cocina o todo lo que gira en torno a ese espacio. MODUS no es un destino final, sino sólo una etapa de un viaje que se renueva completamente cada día.

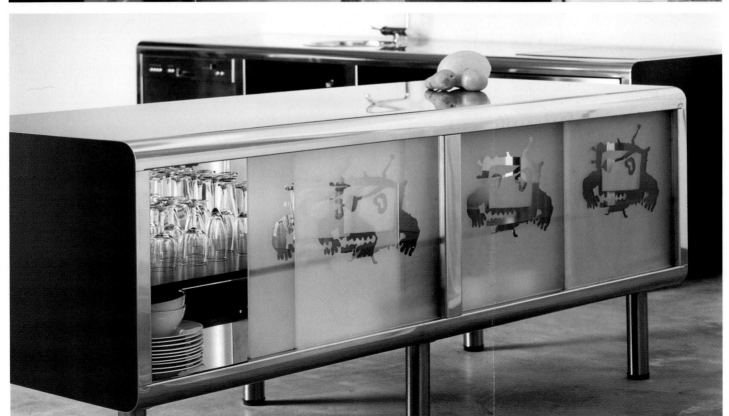

X99
Designed by Ana Motjer & Oliver Schneider
Made by ROYAL FAMILY
www.royalfamily-designlabor.de

Royal Family_design labor was founded about seven years ago by Ana Motjer and Oliver Schneider.The idea for Royal Family originated through various projects for which the members of Royal Family called upon their collective and diverse experience in the areas of furniture, product, set, and communication design. Royal Family is grounded in the laboratory concept perceiving design work as an experiment to find new forms and means of expression.

Royal Family se creó hace siete años porlos diseñadores Ana Motjet y Oliver Schneider. El concepto de diseño de Royal Family es una mezcla de las aventuras profesionales de ambos diseñadores en campos como el diseño de producto, de mobiliario y marketing. Royal Family se basa en un concepto "laboratorio" que considera el diseño como una experimentación para encontrar nuevas formas de expresión.

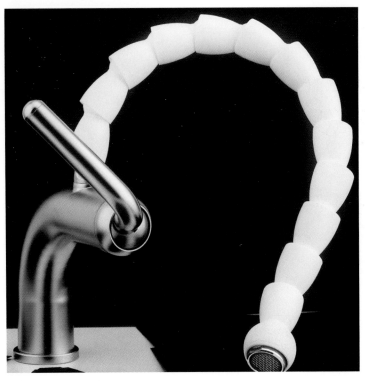

MOMBO_STEEL
Designed by Davide Vercelli
Made by RITMONIO
www.ritmonio.it

MOMBO_STEEL is a single lever mixer for kitchen with turning and articulated spout. The spout can be made on tecnopolimer or aluminium.

MOMBO_STEEL es un mezclador de palanca para cocina con canalón flexible y articulado. El canalón se fabrica en aluminio y otros materiales.

SOVIORE
Designed by Vico Magistretti
Made by SCHIFFINI
www.schiffini.it

Well-balanced dimensions, traditional materials used on technological and modern structures, and maximum accuracy in details make SOVIORE an elegant and up-to-date kitchen.

Dimensiones perfectamente estudiadas, materiales tradicionales usados sobre estructuras tecnológicamente modernas y un cuidado hasta el último detalle hacen de SOVIORE una elegante cocina muy actual.

JAIMACA
Designed by Jorge Pensi
Made by AMAT-3
www.amat-3.com

Frame in tubular steel, chromed or finished in metalic polyester; swivel seat available in two options:
- Cast aluminium, polished and anodised.
- Solid varnished beech wood; colours according to sample collection. The wooden versions are 2 cm higher than indicated.

Esructura de tubo de acero cromado o pintado con poliéster metalizado; asiento giratorio en dos opciones:
- Aluminio fundido, pulido y anodizado.
- Madera maciza de haya barnizada; colores según muestrario. Las versiones de madera son 2 cm más altas que las indicadas.

SPLASH TABLE 5 STAR
Designed by Jorge Pensi
Made by AMAT-3
www.amat-3.com

Base in polished anodised cast aluminium central column in polished anodised aluminiom tube. The SPLASH table base includes adjustable SPLASH or DISK polypropylene feet; colours according to sample collection.
Tabletops according to sample collection:
- Stainless steel
- Laminates
- Compact laminate indoor / outdoor
- Varnished wood

Base de aluminiofundido, pulido y anodizado. Eje central de tubo de aluminio pulido y anodizado. Dispone de Niveladores modelo SPLASH o DISK de polipropileno; colores según muestrario:
- Acero inoxidable
- Laminados
- Compacto exterior / interior
- Maderas barnizadas

SPLASH ARMACHAIR
Designed by Jorge Pensi
Made by AMAT-3
www.amat-3.com

Frame in anodised aluminium tube. Seat support in polished injected aluminium. Seat and back in recyclable polypropylene, colours according to sample.

Estructura de tubo de aluminio anodizado. Soporte para el asiento en aluminio inyectado y pulido. Asiento y respaldo en polipropileno reciclable; colores según muestrario.

QUADRA
Designed by Arrital
Made by ARRITAL CUCINE
www.arritalcucine.com

The idea of this design is to bring together the kitchen and lounge in a single room, a symbol of the evolution of the "house" concept. Teak is the "leitmotiv" in which the solidity of the wood provides a contrast against the luminous "mirror" effect lacquered panes. QUADRA is characterized by genuine teak plywood doors with a choice of either teak or aluminium handles.

La idea de este diseño es incorporar la cocina y zona de estar en un único espacio, símbolo de la evolución del concepto "casa" . La madera de teca es el "leitmotiv" donde la solidez de la madera se compara con la luminosidad de los cristales lacados, efecto "espejo". QUADRA se caracterizado por una puerta contrachapada en verdadera madera de teca , los tiradores pueden ser de madera de teca o aluminio.

CLINO ONCE AGAIN
Designed by Mario Mazzer
Made by MAGIS
www.magisdesign.com

Minimalist retractable wall table, ideal for keeping the small kitchens tidy.
Material: frame in stainless steel tube.
Top in Werzalit.

Mesa de pared de diseño minimalista, es ideal para manterner el orden en cocinas de espacio reducido.
Material: marco de tubo de acero inoxidable.
Tablero en Werzalit.

AIDA TABLE
Designed by Richard Sapper
Made by MAGIS
www.magisdesign.com

MAGIS has created this beautiful and simple collection of folding tables. Once folded it takes up very little space and can be kept in any corner. Suitable for outdoor use.
Materials: Weighted base in standard injection-moulded polyamide. Frame in steel tube cataphoretically-treated, painted in polyester powder. Top in Werzalit.

MAGIS nos presenta la colección de mesas plegables AIDA. Son perfectas para cualquier rincón de la casa incluso en exteriores.
Materiales: la base fabricada en poliamida ha sido modelada por inyección y pintada con poliéster en polvo. El tablero es de Werzalit.

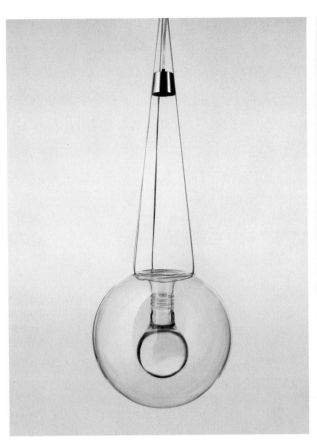

BOMBAY SAPPHIRE LIGHT
Designed by The Bombay Sapphire Foundation
Made by PAUL COCKSEDGE
www.paulcocksedge.co.uk

The design involves pouring gin and tonic into a light bulb-shaped vessel and shining UV light onto the chandelier. Switched on, the clear translucent liquid is transformed into an incredible glowing blue colour.
The liquid becomes the light!
Dimensions:
30cmx30cmx30cm (glass globe)

El diseño implica verter un gintònic en el jarrón con forma de bombilla. Apagamos las luces y enfocamos el jarrón con una luz ultravioleta. El líquido translúcido se transforma en una luz de color azul brillante.
¡La luz proviene del líquido!
Dimensiones:
30cmx30cmx30cm (globo de cristal)

HUGONET SUD
Designed by Pascal Mourgue
Made by HUGONET
www.kettalgroup.com

This table by HUGONET is made from an aluminium frame painted with polyester powder paint. Ideally it can be folded away at any time to leave the kitchen completely free of obstacles.

Esta mesa de la firma HUGONET está fabricada en perfil de aluminio pintado con pintrua poliéster en polvo. Ideal para plegar en cualquier momento dejando la cocina libre de obstáculos.

BOX ONE SYSTEM & SPACE SYSTEM
Designed by Schiffini
Made by SCHIFFINI
www.schiffini.it

SCHIFFINI unveils this immaculate kitchen which is full of surprises. Every drawer is fitted with a return mechanism and a safety catch to prevent the drawer accidentally coming out. The sides and the back of the drawer units are made from naturally extruded anodized aluminium. The base is in transparent 5mm thick tempered safety glass which complies with the established European safety standards as regards kitchen furniture. The metallic triple sliding drawer tracks are particularly strong and guarantee more than 40,000 extractions with loads of up to 80kg per drawer, in addition to being fitted with a return mechanism.
Drawer units are available in 165, 180, 195 and 210 cm widths.

SCHIFFINI nos presenta esta inmaculada cocina llena de sorpresas. Cada cajón está dotado de mecanismo de retorno y de un tope de seguridad, a fin de impedir que se salga accidentalmente. Los laterales y la pared trasera de los cajones son de aluminio extruido anodizado natural. El fondo es de un vidrio templado transparente de seguridad, que mide 5 mm de espesor. Dichos vidrios cumplen con todo lo establecido en las normas europeas de seguridad, en materia de muebles de cocina. Las guías metálicas de extracción triple son particularmente sólidas y garantizan más de 40.000 extracciones, con cargas de hasta 80 Kg por cajón. Además, poseen mecanismo de retorno.
Medidas de los cajones, de 165, 180, 195 y 210 cm de ancho.

MODUS
Designed by Paolo Nava & Fabio Casiraghi
Made by BINOVA
www.binova.com

Therefore, the curtains have been conceived to turn the architecture of the kitchen and home into an architectural element that changes the perspective of space and focuses one's attention on the worktops.

MODUS nos demuestra que el uso de los bastidores, concebidos para transformar la arquitectura de la cocina y de la casa, como un elemento arquitectónico, puede modificar la prospectiva del espacio, capaces de concentrar la atención sobre las encimeras.

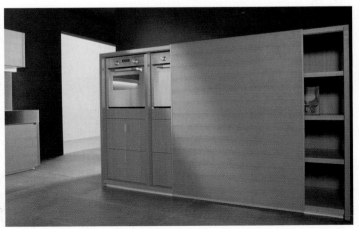

COMO
Designed by Leicht
Made by LEICHT
www.leicht.de

Casual elegance and comfortable living characterise the kitchen model COMO, a modern country house kitchen with an elaborate profile frames front. The two-colour surface structure allows for the edges to be carefully finished by hand. Thus profiles and panels have an individual patina, protected by a double application of transparent lacquer. The surround accessories offer everything that is needed for the arrangement of a modern country house kitchen: for instance, pilaster with recessed plinth, an elegant cornice, glass fronted cupboards with glazing bars or a special light blender.

Elegancia, que inspira confianza, y una sensación confortable de habitabilidad caracterizan a la cocina COMO, dándole un moderno aire de cocina casa de campo, con una puerta de cuarterones moldurados. La elaboración en dos tonalidades de la superficie permite el lijado a mano. El moldurado y los plafones reciben, de este modo, una pátina, protegida por la doble capa de su lacado transparente. El entorno ofrece todo cuanto se necesita para la realización de una moderna cocina en estilo casa de campo: por ejemplo, pilastras con retranqueo de zócalo, una cornisa elegante, ventanas con listoncillos para los armarios de cristal o una especial regleta de luz.

SKIPPING STOOL
Designed by Karim Rashid
Made by BONALDO
www.karimrashid.com
www.bonaldo.com

Thanks to its light and elegant shape it can be used both in domestic and contract environments, wherever there is a need to quickly change or transform spaces.
Skipping's "S" shape lends it harmony and its high back. together with the comfortable footrest, are an invitation to relax. Skipping can furthermore be regulated in height thanks to a gas piston mechanism. The frame in chrome-plated steel, the seat and back are upholstered with expanded polyurethane and covered with leather or skai.

Gracias a su forma ligera y elegante, éste taburete puede ser usado en la cocina como en cualquier otro lugar de la casa, así como en oficinas y lugares de trabajo .
La forma en "S" del taburete SKIPPING aporta armonía y hace que su respaldo sea muy alto. La altura se puede regular gracias a su pistón de gas. Está fabricado en acero cromado de color plata y el asiento y respaldo se han tapizado en poliuretano y cubiertos de cuero o skai.

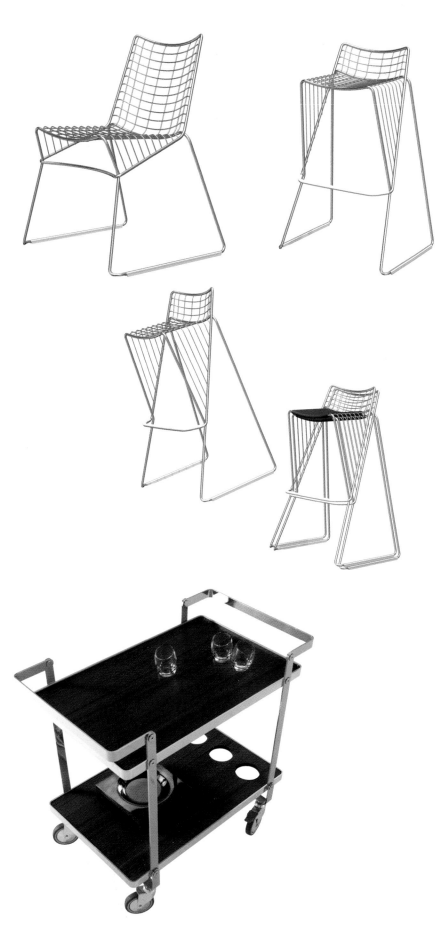

STRINGS CHAIR, HIGH STOOL & LOW STOOL
Designed by Azumi
Made by AZUMI
www.azumi.co.uk

Wire mesh stacking chair and stools. The design achieves high production-efficiency by using just three patterns of bent wires to create mesh structure. The chair can have seat and back pads to provide decent comfort.
Structure: Stainless Steel / Powder Coated Steel
Stool: W=600 D=455 H=820/920 SH=660/760
Chair: W=590 D=515 H=790 SH=455

AZUMI nos presenta esta colección de sillas y taburetes metálicos apilables fabricados en alambre. El diseño de alta calidad ha sido realizado utilizando tan sólo tres modelos de alambre distintos para crear la estructura en forma de malla. La silla también se fabrica con asientos o respaldos con relleno para aportar comodidad y comfort.
Estructura: Acero inoxidable / Acero cubierto en polvo
Taburete: W=600 D=455 H=820/920 SH=660/760
Silla: W=590 D=515 H=790 SH=455

DESSERTE ROSET
Designed by Frederic Ruyant
Made by FREDERIC RUYANT
www.fredericruyant.com

This occasional table in stainless steel with a non-slip wooden table top comes from French designer Frederic Ruyant. Wheels enable meals to be transported from the kitchen to anywhere in the house and it can also be used as an improvised drinks bar at any party.

El diseñador francés Frederic Ruyant nos presenta esta mesa auxiliar fabricada en acero inoxidable y con tablas de madera antideslizante. Las ruedas nos facilitan el transporte de comida de la cocina a cualquier rincón de la casa, también se puede convertir en un impro-visado minibar en cualquier fiesta.

living cool!

salones de ensueño

The lounge is the heart of any home and one of the most frequented rooms in the house. It's important therefore to make sure this room has a welcoming ambience and is both comfortable and practical to support communal living and family life. Over the next few pages a wide range of designs are to be seen which will, without doubt, fulfil these aforementioned requirements, unconventional sofas, chaise longues and a variety of ingenious and practical occasional pieces to help create just the right ambiance.

La sala de estar es el corazón de la vivienda y una de las zonas más concurridas. Hay que procurar que sea una estancia acogedora con un ambiente confortable y funcional donde se facilite la convivencia y la vida familiar. En las siguientes páginas, se muestra un amplio despliegue de diseños, que sin duda facilitará lo anteriormente mencionado, sofás poco convencionales, chaise lounge y variedad de complementos ingeniosos y prácticos permitirán recrear estos ambientes.

LOFT
Designed by Arketipo
Made by ARKETIPO
www.arketipo.com

The major success of the Loft sofa, presented at 2003 Milan Fair, has suggested the exploration of new formal arrangements. By adding lateral elements and chaise longues to the sofa range, the compositional potential of the system has been expanded to the maximum.
The mechanism, which with a simple movement makes it possible to modify the depth of the seating area, remains the priority and original feature of this sofa system, an innovative invention which offers a superior degree of comfort and enables the entire sofa concept to be experienced in an extremely personal manner.

El sofá Loft presentado en la feria del mueble de Milán en el año 2003, fué uno de los grandes exitos de Arketipo. Integrar sillones y elementos laterales a la estructura del sofá ha ayudado a elevar al producto a su máxima expresión.
El mecanismo, que con un simple movimiento hace posible modificar la profundidad del asiento, es un innovador invento que ofrece un grado superior de comfort y convierte al típico sofá en un objeto con el que experimentar de una manera muy personalizada.

OVAL TABLE
Designed by Tord Boontje Collection
Made by MOROSO
www.moroso.it

Beautiful oval dining table designed by Tord Boontje for Italian company Moroso. Thanks to the exquisite design this table top is pretty enough without the need for any decoration.

Preciosa mesa de comedor de forma ovalada diseñada por Tord Boontje para la firma italiana Moroso. La superficie de la mesa es tan bonita gracias a su diseño que no nos hace falta adornar la mesa con nada más.

TONELLI LOTUS
Designed by Karim Rashid
Made by KARIM RASHID
www.karimrashid.com

Shelf unit designed using different types of glass: acid, smoked, and tempered. The legs are in aluminium. Exquisitely designed by Karim Rashid and perfect for any combined lounge and dining room.

Estantería diseñada con distintos tipos de cristal: ácido, ahumado y templado. Las patas son de aluminio. Perfecta para cualquier salón-comedor y diseñada exquisitamente por Karim Rashid.

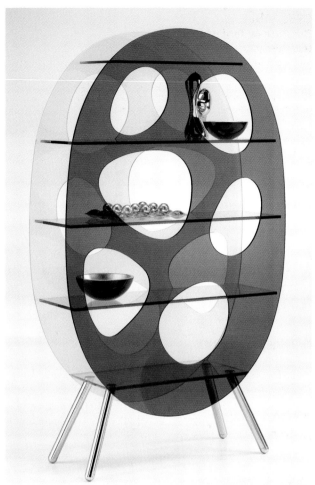

T-UKIYO
Designed by Kazuhiko Tomita
Made by MOROSO
www.moroso.it

We are immediately transported to the Far East by these occasional tables decorated with traditional Japanese kimonos, the fabrics of which have been covered in polyester resin to create the table tops. Floral motives have been a symbol of the Japanese culture for centuries, something which inspired Moroso to create these wonderfully decorative and useful items for our lounges.

Estas mesitas auxiliares nos transportan de inmediato al lejano Oriente gracias a los estampados de los tradicionales kimonos japoneses, tejidos que han sido cubiertos por resina de poliéster para fabricar el tablero. Los motivos florales han sido utilizados por la cultura japonesa durante siglos, por eso Moroso se inspira y nos regala esta maravilla decorativa y útil para nuestro salón.

SMOCK
Designed by Patricia Urquiola
Made by MOROSO
www.moroso.it

Patricia Urquiola has an innate capacity to design objects with a strong connotation, which revolve around the upholstered families. A new look at the hammock style, presented at the Ideal House exhibition in Cologne; the ideal companion to the Smock armchair presented at last year´s Milan Furniture Show. It displays the same exploration of solids and voids, comfort and luxury, that distinguishes Urquiola´s work. This sophisticated, elegant sofa uses a light, stylised design centred around the draping over the ring-shaped armrests. The unusual feature of a full-length zip is for removing the cover and for joining different materials.

Patricia Urquiola ha diseñado para la firma italiana Moroso este fantástico sofá, mezclando muchos conceptos: lujo, comfort, vacíos, llenos... Este sofisticado y elegante sofá se caracteriza por los decorativos fruncidos que se han realizado alrededor de los brazos en forma de anillo.

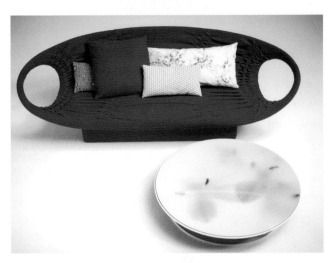

SULTAN & ZELDA
Designed by Ibride
Made by IBRIDE
www.ibride.fr

From Ibride we are presented with these elegant occasional tables with animal legs. Perfect for the most modern and slightly outrageous and makes for an ideal home telephone table.

Ibride nos presenta sus elegantes mesas auxiliares con patas en forma de animales. Perfectos para los más modernos y atrevidos, ideal para poner el teléfono en casa.

SARUYAMA ISLAND
Designed by Toshiyuki Kita
Made by MOROSO
www.moroso.it

The Saruyama collection of sofas and stools, although designed almost 20 years ago by Moroso, is one of the icons of contemporary design. Very practical but also an exquisite design inspired by the shape of any archipelago. Designed with fairly spacious rooms in mind, this modular system gives us complete freedom when it comes to decorating our lounge and will doubtless bestow a great deal of personality and an almost organic character upon the room itself.

El conjunto de sofás y taburetes Saruyama es uno de los iconos del diseño contemporáneo, diseñado hace casi 20 años por Moroso. Muy funcional pero con un diseño exquisito inspirado en las formas de cualquier archipiélago. Pensado para los espacios amplios este sistema modular nos permite total libertad a la hora de decorar nuestro salón, al que sin duda alguna le daremos mucha personalidad y un carácter casi orgánico.

TAVOLINA
Designed by Ibride
Made by IBRIDE
www.ibride.fr

A floral print which appears to shine in the dark decorates this pretty little lounge table, just perfect for in front of the sofa.
Dimensions: 36x80x45 cm

Estampados florales que parecen brillar en la oscuridad para esta preciosa mesita para el salón, perfecta para poner frente al sofá.
Dimensiones: 36x80x45 cm

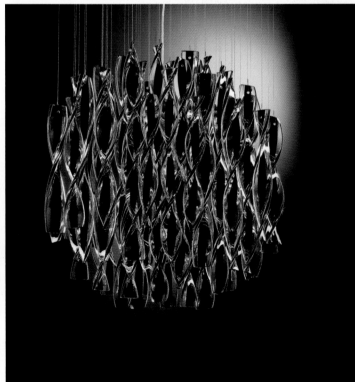

AURA
Designed by Axo light
Made by AXO LIGHT
www.axolight.it

Waves of light, bands of color, crystal plays: silky hair, choppy seas, glittering objects inspired by the hydrodynamic shapes of marine animals. In the Aura collection, glass is produced and finished off completely by hand, using the traditional techniques of the Murano masters.

Oleadas de luz, haces de color, juegos de cristal: cabellos sedosos, océano encrespado, objetos brillantes inspirados en las formas hidrodinámicas de los animales marinos. Los vidrios de la colección Aura están realizados y acabados uno por uno completamente a mano, utilizando técnicas tradicionales de los maestros de Murano.

DRAGONFLY CHAISE LONGUE
Designed by Karim Rashid
Made by BONALDO
www.karimrashid.com
www.bonaldo.com

DRAGONFLY is a completely new and unconventional chaise-longue. With its essential shape and the possibility of ordering it in a two-color version, it goes beyond the classic idea of an easy chair offering a sparkling and fun article. DRAGONFLY has another advantage: it offers two excellent seats – an easy chair and a chaise-longue – that occupy the space of one. These characteristics will certainly make it popular with the younger crowd that pays increasing attention to detail and to the purchase of furniture with a truly functional design.

DRAGONFLY es una chaise-longue completamente nueva y nada convencional. Con su forma esencial y la posibilidad de elegir entre una versión bicolor, BONALDO va más allá del concepto típico de la silla para el salón, ofreciendo un divertido e impactante producto. DRAGONFLY tiene otra ventaja: ofrece dos excellentes asientos en uno, una silla normal y corriente y una chaise-longue ocupando el mismo espacio. Estas características la hacen muy popular entre los clientes más jovenes que ponen especial atención a este tipo de detalles a la hora de comprar mobiliario con un diseño funcional.

CLOSER
Designed by Tord Boontje
Made by MOROSO
www.moroso.it

Outsized upholstered elements that combine the opulent forms of metaphysical seating elements with the comforting forms of our memory. Forms that make their presence felt, the textile covers with striking floral graphic motifs were also designed by Boontje. Wooden frame covered with stress-resistant polyurethane foam at varied densities and polyester fiber. Seat cushion of armchair in stress resistant polyurethane foam at varied densities and polyester fiber. Standard feet, screwed to the frame, in black polypropylen.

Este sillón, tapizado con tejidos de impactantes gráficos florales, aporta color a nuestro salón y comfort para los momentos de relax. Construído sobre una base de madera y relleno de poliuretano de distintas densidades hace de este sillón una producto muy resistente y duradero. El cojín del asiento también ha sido fabricado con los mismos materiales además de fibra de poliéster. Las patas, atornilladas al marco de madera de la base, son de polipropileno negro.

T-BON BON
Designed by Tord Boontje
Made by MOROSO
www.moroso.it

A series of tables of different heights – side table, low table, coffee table – decorated with delicate floral motifs. Ultra-sophisticated and precious in the Corian® versions featuring dye-sublimation printing (a technique by which the ink permeates the material).

MOROSO nos presenta esta preciosa colección de mesas de varias medidas decoradas con delicados motivos florales. Ultra-sofisticada y preciosa en las versiones Corian® con impresiones por sublimación (técnica en la que la tinta impregna el material).

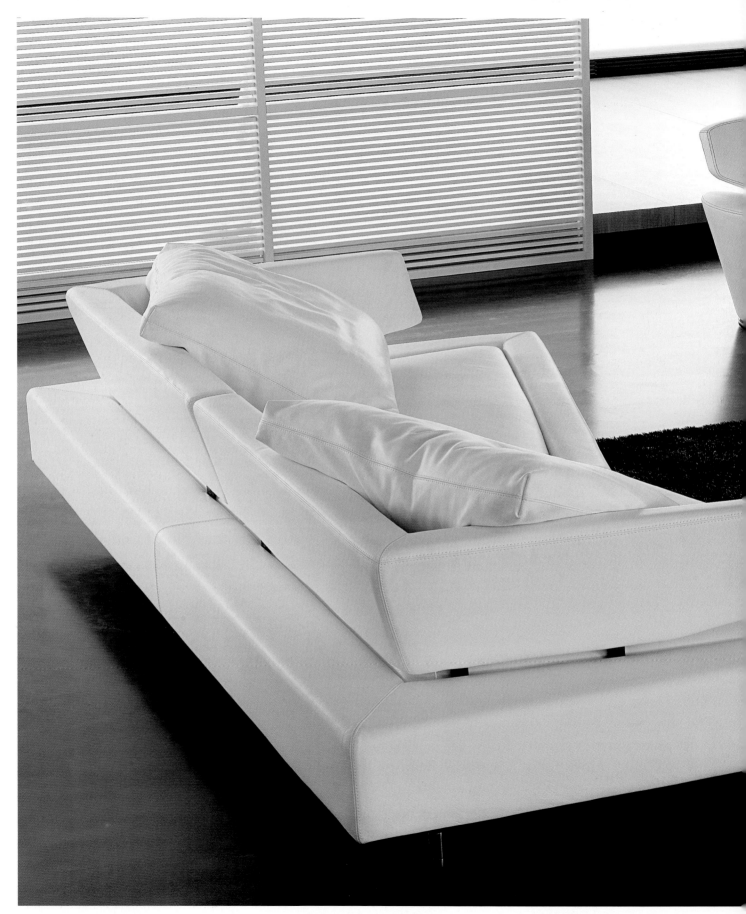

MUST
Designed by
Made by ARKETIPO
www.arketipo.com

MUST
Designed by Arketipo
Made by ARKETIPO
www.arketipo.com

The striking feature of the MUST seating system is the special wedge shape of the elements. They are also equipped with a clever functional mechanism, so that the depth of the seat can be modified simply by sliding the backrest forward, transforming the sofa from a totally relaxed, informal mode to a more formal classic aspect. The wedge-shaped elements can also be combined with an original round pouf.

La caracterísica más destacable de sistema de asientos MUST es la forma de cuña de todos sus elementos. Están equipados con un mecanismo funcional inteligente, de modo que la profundidad del asiento puede ser modificada simplemente deslizando el respaldo, transformando el sofá de un modo más informal a un aspecto clásico más formal. También se pueden combinar con un original reposapiés redondo.

VICTOR & VICTORIA CHAIRS
Designed by Dondoli & Pocci
Made by BONALDO
www.bonaldo.it

The peculiarly rounded shape of the back is what sets these new chairs apart. The slightly inclined legs lend grace and lightness. The upholstered seat and removable covers make them suited to different home environments, from the dining to the living room. The frame of Victor is in chrome-plated steel and the covers can be in fabric or leather, while Victoria is completely covered in leather.

Lo que hace que estas sillas sean únicas en su clase es la original forma redondeada de su respaldo. Las patas, ligeramente inclinadas, aportan gracia y ligereza a la silla. Los tapicería y las fundas intercambiables nos permiten colocarlas en cualquier ambiente de la casa, desde el comedor a la sala de estar. La estructura de VICTOR es de acero cromado plateado y las fundas son de tela o piel, mientras que VICTORIA viene totalment forrada de piel.

TRANSFORM
Designed by For Use
Made by MOROSO
www.moroso.it

Linear aestheticism, formal neatness and a typically eastern rationalism mark the design of FOR USE, a Croatian design studio that has designed a small armchair for Moroso with a back with two manual movements.

Aesteticismo lineal, pulcritud formal y un racionalismo típico de FOR USE, un estudio de diseño Croata, ha diseñado este pequeño sofá para MOROSOS con un respaldo con dos movimientos totalmente manuales.

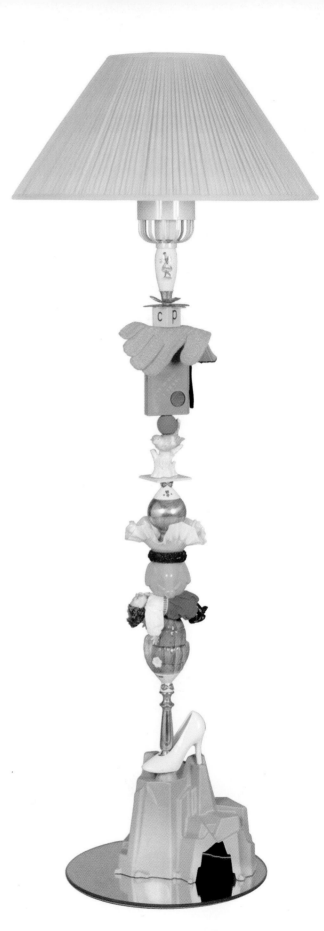

THE KEBAB LAMP
Designed by Committe
Made by COMMITTE
www.gallop.co.uk

The Committee KEBAB LAMP stands are made by skewering a collection of found objects, antiques and other miscellany no longer in use with the aim of delighting the viewer with an explosion of colour and reference. Built as a totem of improbably varied materials, the lamps are carefully composed to contain stories and meanings amongst the eclectic objects they include and consequently each lamp is unique and filled with pieces from different eras that allude to the constant turning of fashion and style.

The concept behind the lamps was born of Committee's interest in the way people relate to and value objects and the lamps play with this sense of value as fine porcelain and plastic come together to form a sculptural composition with its own integrity. The lamps are also intended to be explorations of 'taste', whilst simultaneously referring to the consumption of material goods and the inevitable waste this produces. Of course they can also light your room...

Committee is very pleased to add that the lamps won the UK Elle Decoration/Observer Design Award for Best in Lighting 2004. In 2005 they were selected to appear in the German Design Council's "Interior Innovations Award" at Cologne after which a collection of lamps was presented at Dilmos design gallery for the Milan Furniture Fair 05 and at Cibone design store for Tokyo Design Week 05.

Las lámparas KEBAB de Committee han sido diseñadas a partir de una colección de objetos reciclados, algunos encontrados en anticuarios y otros en la basura, con el ánimo de provocar en el espectardor una explosión de color y recuerdos del pasado. Construídas como una especie "totems", las lámparas contienen historias, nos transmiten mensajes y nos provocan sensaciones, atacan directamente a nuestros recuerdos. Cada lámpara es única, no existen dos iguales, llenas de piezas de diferentes eras que aluden al constante cambio de la moda y el diseño.

El concepto de estas lámparas nació del interés de Committee por la manera en la que las personas valoran sus objetos personales, las lámparas juegan con esta sensación de valor: porcelna fina y plástico se juntan para formar una composición escultórica con su propia integridad. Las lámparas intentan explorar el "buen gusto" y por supuesto su función es la de iluminar...

Comittee ha ganado varios galardones durante los últimos años como el UK Elle Decoration/Observer Design Award a la mejor iluminación 2004. En el año 2005 fueron seleccionados para el German Design Council's "Interior Innovations Award" en Colonia, despues de que su colección de lámparas fuera presentada en la galería Dilmos durante la feria del mueble de Milán y en la tienda Cibon Design durante la semana del diseño en Tokio.

LEI CHAIR
Designed by Dondoli & Pocci
Made by BONALDO
www.bonaldo.it

Simple and organic design, together with structural lightness and comfort makes the chairs of the LEI collection the ideal products to lend a touch of liveliness to home and professional environments.

Already available in different versions and numerous finishes, in 2006 Bonaldo presents a new version with seat and back in oak for which a highly technological material was used: 3-D laminate thanks to which accentuated concave and convex shapes can be obtained. This provides an additional opportunity to enjoy the unique characteristics of wood – the grain, the warmth of the surfaces, the feeling of well-being and comfort that wood conveys – without having to forego the functional and aesthetic needs of a contemporary lifestyle.

Diseño simple y orgánico, junto a una estructura ligera y comfortable hace que las sillas de la colección LEI sean ideales tanto para el uso en el hogar como para ambientes profesionales.

Disponible en distintas versiones y numerosos acabados, Bonaldo prentó en el 2006 una nueva versión con asiento y respaldo en madera de roble para la que se utilizó un material de alta tecnología: laminado 3-D, con el que se acenturaron y se obtuviero formas más cóncavas y convexas. Esta nueva tecnología nos da la oportunidar de disfrutar de las características únicas de esta madera - el grano, la calidez de las texturas, la sensación de comfort que la madera nos ofrece - sin olvidar la funcionalidad y la estética que se necesita en el estilo de vida contemporáneo.

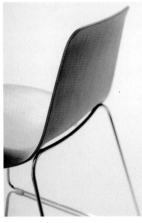

RIPPLE CHAIR
Designed by Ron Arad
Made by MOROSO
www.moroso.it

The frame of RIPPLE CHAIR is made of white polished and natural injection-moulded thermoplastic to highlight the design in relief that is reminiscent of the traces left by sea waves on sand. The circular aperture of the seat, the lightness and softness of the lines, the sturdiness of the material used and its stackability make Ripple Chair particularly suitable for both domestic and public spaces.

La estructura de la RIPPLE CHAIR ha sido moldeada por inyección termoplástica para destacar el diseño del relieve que nos recuerda a los rastros dejados por las olas del mar en la arena. La apertura circular del asiento, la ligereza y suavidad de las líneas, la fuerza del material usado y su capacidad de amontonarse hace que la RIPPLE Chair pueda ser utilizada tanto para espacios domésticos como para públicos.

CABINET F
Designed by Jonas Bohlin and Thomas Sandell
Made by ASPLUND
www.asplund.org

Pure lines for this sophisticated immaculate white bookcase complete with doors, ideal for storing books in the lounge at the same time protecting them from dust thanks to protective glass doors.

Líneas puras para esta mueble estantería en inmaculado color blanco con puertas, es ideal para guardar libros en nuestro salón de una manera sofisticada protegiéndolos del polvo gracias al cristal protector de las puertas.

DUNA
Designed by Rodrigo Torres
Made by DOMODINAMICA
www.domodinamica.com

The seat is made of polyurethane resins cold foamed in die and is covered with elastic fabrics. The base is in curved laminated wood - polished lacquering. Placed side by side offers a sweet succession of dunes, adjusting themselves to our body and following its movements.

Este sillón está fabricado con resinas de poliuretano transformadas en esponja y forrado con tejidos elásticos. Las patas son de madera curvada laminada. Colocadas una al lado de la otra nos da la sensación de una dulce sucesión de dunas, ajustándose a nuestro cuerpo y siguiendo sus movimientos.

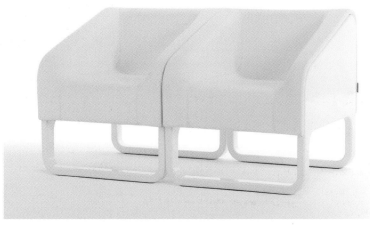

MIST
Designed by Rodrigo Torres
Made by DOMODINAMICA
www.domodinamica.com

The MIST armchair designed by Rodrigo Torres for Domodinamica is made of polyurethane resins cold foamed in die and is covered with elastic fabrics. You can position them side by side. The sweet mantle gives to the armchair a charme recalling lightness and confort.

Domodinamica de la mano del diseñador Rodrigo Torres nos presenta este sillón de espuma realizado con resinas de poliuretano y forrado con tejidos elásticos. Si jugamos con ellos colocándolos uno al lado del otro obtemenos una ligera calidez y sensación de confort.

LEM 90
Designed by A & H Van Onck
Made by MAGIS
www.magisdesign.com

Table adjustable in height.
Material: frame in chromed steel. Top in MDF with polymeric cover, cherrywood or beech.

Mesa de altura ajustable.
Material: estructura de acero cromado. Tablero en MDF, madera de cerezo o haya.

BIG BOX
Designed by Enrico Cesana
Made by SPHAUS
www.sphaus.com

BIG BOX is a container system based on four modules: three linear modules and one-L-shaped module which can be put together in variety of different ways.
Available in two depths, 65 cm and 43cm, Big Box is made of matt lacquered MDF. The large sliding drawers may be fitted with a range of accesories.

BIG BOX es conjunto de cajoneras basado en cuatro módulos: tres módulos lineales y uno en forma de L.
Disponible en profundidades distintas, 65 cm y 43 cm, BIG BOX está hecho de MDF laqueado mate. Los cajones vienen con una gran variedad de accesorios.

APPLE
Designed by Dodo Arslan
Made by SPHAUS

www.sphaus.com

Two unusual details help to increase the seat´s comfort: firstly, the fact that the chair gently closes when prompted by a person´sweight with the aid of a special hinge structure, and secondly, because APPLE is a rocking chair.

Dos detalles inusales ayudan a incrementar el comfort de esta silla: primero de todo, el hecho que que la silla se cierra cuando una persona se sienta "abrazándola" suavemente, y en segundo lugar, porque APPLE es una silla mecedora.

SKIP LOUNGE EASY CHAIR
Designed by Karim Rashid
Made by BONALDO
www.karimrashid.com
www.bonaldo.com

Like the stool Skipping, the easy chair SKIP LOUNGE is a variation on the theme of the Skip chair Bonaldo presented in 2005.

Skip Lounge shares the same limited size and light weight of the rest of the Skip seat family. Thanks to an ample variety of coverings it can be positioned in different home or public environments, adapting itself to the different colors and accessories, from single shades to floral patterns, in combination or as a free-standing item.

The frame is in chrome-plated or varnished steel, the seat and back covered with leather or fabric.

Igual que el taburete Skipping, la silla SKIP LOUNGE es una variación de la silla Skip que bonaldo presentó en el 2005.

SKIP LOUNGE comparte las mismas proporciones y ligereza que el resto de la familia Skip. Gracias a una amplia variedad de fundas, la silla puede utilizarse tanto en espacios domésticos como en lugares públicos, ya que se adapta a infinidad de colores y accesorios, desde colores planos a motivos florales.

La estructura es de acero cromado plateado o acero varnizado, el asiento y el respaldo van tapizados con piel o tela.

PLAT
Designed by Arketipo
Made by ARKETIPO
www.arketipo.com

PLAT is a system of seats consisting of a wide range of modular elements which, apart from offering a high degree of comfort due to the use of down cushions combined with an internal spring system, also allow for "inventing" ever-varying formal solutions. The platform is the original element: a spatial extension of the system that lends itself for being used freely either as a bench or an informal seat. The platform can be fitted out with a series of container elements: trays and book rests in various sizes, all made in crystal and steel.

PLAT es un sistema de asientos que consiste en un amplio abanico de elementos modulares los cuales ofrecen un alto grado de comfort debido al uso de cojines bajos. La base es el elemento estrella de este sofá que puede ser usado como un banco o un asiento informal, además podemos aplicar a la base varios elementos muy útiles como reposa libros en varias medidas, todos fabricados en acero y cristal.

BOSON & BOSON TABLE
Designed by Matali Crasset
Made by ARTIFORT
www.artifort.com

What defines matter? According to physical theories from the 60's matter is strongly connected with "Higgs Boson" a particle or range of particles that shape substance. The concept of the chair is: Working with synthetic material, visual substance, weightlessness.
The first objective in creating the chair was to optimize applied material to offer a new and plain seating system; minimizing the synthetic material to obtain an ideal balance between form and function.

¿Qué define la materia? Según las teorías físicas que se investigaron en los años 60, la materia está estrechamente relacionada con "Hiss Boson" una partícula o variedad de partículas que dan forma a algo. El concepto de la silla es: Trabajar con materiales sintéticos, sustancia visual, ingravidez.
El objetivo principal al crear la sill fué optimizar los materiales aplicados para ofrecer un sistema de asientos nuevo y de líneas simples; la reducción al mínimo del material sintético para obtener un equilibrio idean entre forma y funcionalidad.

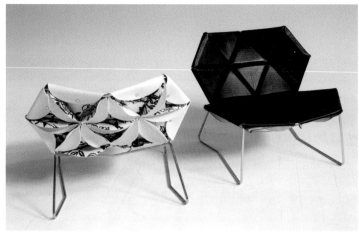

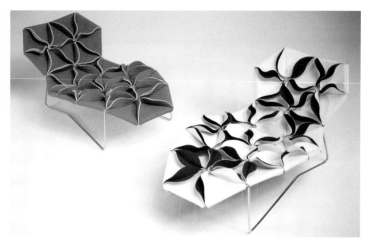

ANTIBODI
Designed by Patricia Urquiola
Made by MOROSO
www.moroso.it

Seeking a new shape for a non-upholstered seating element, a lounge chair or a chaise longue, the design blossoms from a "cellular" genesis of petals sewn in triangular shapes, creating ample patterns. The lightly padded petals feature reversible materials – felt and wool fabric; wool fabric and leather – which create a supporting cover that is then fixed to a stain-lesssteel metal frame.
The cover creates two very different and striking moods: with the petals facing upwards for a more unconventional, feminine version; or facing downward for a deliberately severe, quilted look.

Buscando una nueva forma para un elemento para sentarse no tapizado, una silla de salón o una chaise-longue, el diseño ANTIBODI florece de una génesis "celular" de pétalos cosidos en formas triangulares. Los pétalos ligeramente acolchados presentan materiales reversibles - fieltro, lana y piel - que crean una funda soporte fijada a una estructura de acero inoxidable. Encontramos dos tipos de funda: con los pétalos hacia arriba huyendo de lo convencional, o hacia abajo para un aspecto más serio y acolchado.

POLDER SOFA
Designed by Hella Jongerius
Made by VITRA
www.vitra.com

In Holland Polder refers to the artificial land reclaimed from the sea by means of dikes and drainage canals. The corpus of the POLDER SOFA is just as low-lying, just as flat, and with just as much emphasis on the horizontal. For it Hella Jongerius chose five carefully selected combinations of colours and fabric qualities, accentuating them with high-tech threads and large buttons made of natural materials.

En Holanda Polder hace referencia a la tierra ganada artificialmente al mar mediante la colocación de diques y zanjas de drenaje. El cuerpo del POLDER SOFA está situado igual de bajo y se presenta igual de plano, resaltando asímismo la línea horizontal. Hella Jongerius eligió para este sofá cinco combinaciones de colores y tapicerías a juego que acentúa con hilo de alta tecnología y grandes botones de materiales naturales.

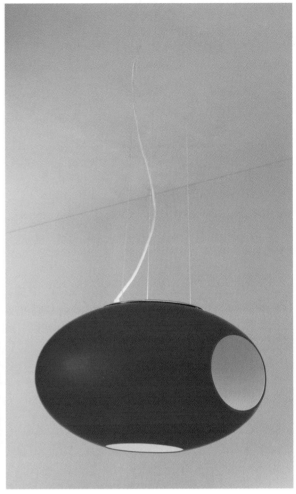

BALL-UP
Designed by Axo light
Made by AXO LIGHT
www.axolight.it

The key to interpreting BALL-UP lamps is emotional, the suggestion of light, shape and color reaches out to the playful part in each of us so that we can interpret and define its shape to our hearts content.
BALL-UP seems to want to keep light to itself, protecting it inside its crystal sphere to release it all at once.

El código de lectura de las lámparas BALL-UP es emocional, la sugestión de luz, de forma y de color llega hasta la parte jocosa de cada uno de nosotros que interpreta y define, a su gusto, la forma.
BALL-UP parece querer quedarse con la luz, protegerla en el interior de su esfera de cristal para luego soltarla de repente.

JAM
Designed by Jan Borchies
Made by IBRIDE
www.ibride.fr

This modern and stunning living room table it's been designed by Jan Borchies for french brand Ibride. Living room table specifications:
Height: 40 cm
Width: 130 cm
Table: 21mm MDF-board & Glass covered with foil
Legs: Aluminium

Ésta fantástica y moderna mesa de salón ha sido diseñada por el diseñador Jan Borchies para la marca francesa Ibride.
Especificaciones:
Altura: 40 cm
Ancho: 130 cm
Tablero: 21 mm MDF y cristal cubierto por hoja de metal
Patas: Aluminio

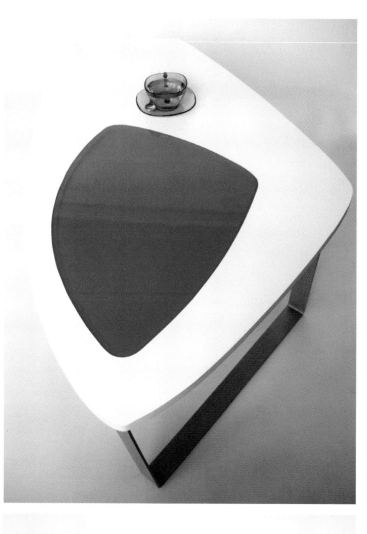

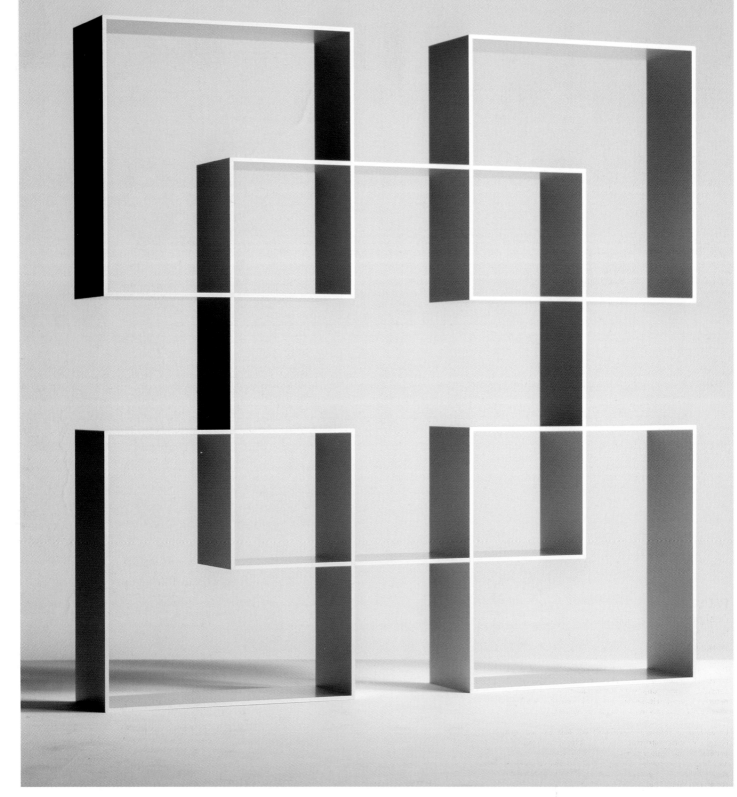

KOSHI
Designed by Axo light
Made by AXO LIGHT
www.axolight.it

The harmony of KOSHI is the result of many contrasts of shapes, colors and materials. The opalescence of blown glass, the glittering reflections of metal, the strong nuances of wood give life to an intriguing play of shades, a sophisticated combination of materials and expert workmanship. The collection is available in hanging, table, floor, wall and ceiling versions in different sizes.

La armonía de KOSHI se apoya en un espeso contraste de formas, de colores y de materiales. La opalescencia del vidrio soplado, los reflejos chispeantes del metal, los matices decididos de la madera dan vida a un intrigante juego de sombras, un sofisticado connubio de materiales y de sabios trabajos. La colección se encuentra disponible en las aplicaciones suspendida, de mesa, de pie, de pared y de techo en diversos tamaños.

PAUSE
Designed by Aziz Sariyer
Made by MOROSO
www.moroso.it

The bookshelf by Aziz Sariyer for Moroso is a one-piece structure made of anodised honeycomb aluminium sandwich panels. Characterised by essential lines and a recurring geometric shape, the bookshelf can act as a space divider or as a multi-purpose container.

La estantería para libros diseñada por Aziz Sariyer para Moroso es una estructura de una sola pieza hecha de paneles de aluminio y panal anonizado. Caracterizado por sus líneas esenciales y una forma geométrica que se repite, la librería puede actuar como separador de ambientes en una misma habitación o como estantería multiuso.

CLAVIUS
Designed by Axo light
Made by AXO LIGHT
www.axolight.it

BERLIN EASY CHAIR
Designed by Stefan Heiliger
Made by BONALDO
www.bonaldo.it

BERLIN, designed by Stefan Heiliger, is an easy chair with a very original shape. When the back is folded over, it forms a 90° angle that provides a comfortable backrest that invites relaxation and conversation; once extended, the seat transforms into a chaise-longue on which one can rest or read a good book. To move the back from the seated to the reclined position all one has to do is pull up and back.

BERLIN, diseñada por Stefan Heiliger, es una silla con una forma muy original. Cuando el respaldo está plegado, forma un ángulo de 90 grados que proporciona un comfortable reposo para la espalda que invita a la relajación y a conversar; una vez se despliega, la silla se transforma en una chaise-longue en la que uno puede descansar o leer un buen libro. Para mover el respaldo de una posición a otra, lo único que tenemos que hacer es tirar hacia arriba o hacia abajo.

Essential design, refined in its linearity, creates a play of light and shade, an alternation of color nuances and reflections that the weft of the diffuser handles with expertise creating atmospheres full of fascination and style in each environment.
The frame is chrome-plated and the diffuser in opaline metacrylate. Clavius is available as a floor, hanging, ceiling and wall lamp in different sizes.

El diseño esencial, refinado en su linealidad, crea un juego de luces y sombras, un alternarse de tonalidades cromáticas y de reflejos que la trama del difusor contrasta con maestría, regalando atmósferas llenas de encanto y estilo en todos los ambientes.
La montura es cromada y el difusor es de meta crilato opalino. La colección está compuesta por la versión suspendida, de tierra, de pared y de techo en diversos tamaños.

C-PHOENIX
Designed by Patricia Urquiola
Made by MOROSO
www.moroso.it

The PHOENIX containers enrich and complete the upholstered systems and seats made of plastic materials. In various dimensions and heights, from the most compact to the most generous, they define and circumscribe the living zone. They are multipurpose, adaptable to any environment, standing against walls or forming an island of sofas, and they certainly make domestic life more pleasant and tidy!

Los armarios PHOENIX se presentan en diferentes dimensiones y alturas, desde el más compacto hasta el más generoso, nos ayudarán a definir y circunscribir nuestro salón. Al estar tapizados, son multiuso y adaptables a cualquier ambiente: de pié contra la pared o formando una isla de sofás, haciendo la vida doméstica más agradable y ordenada.

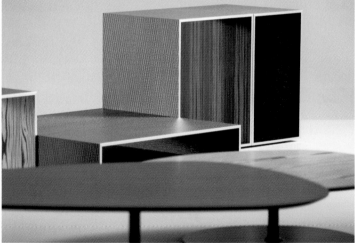

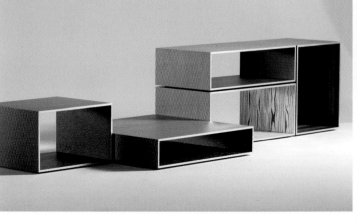

DAYBED
Designed by George Nelson
Made by VITRA
www.vitra.com

George Nelson designed the Daybed to furnish his own weekend home on Long Island. The comfortable seat-cum-recliner serves not only as a sofa or daytime recliner, but with the back removed also doubles up easily as a temporary guest bed. Once again, a superior-quality version of this unpretentious and yet elegant design is now available.

George Nelson diseñó la Daybed para amueblar su propia casa de fin de semana en Long Island. Este cómodo mueble, a medio camino entre el sofá y la tumbona, no sólo es un excelente sofá o una tumbona de día, sino que, una vez retirados los acolchados del respaldo, también se puede utilizar como cama de invitados provisional. Este diseño sin pretensiones y, sin embargo, elegante se vuelve a fabricar en una versión de gran calidad.

NESTING TABLES
Designed by Josef Albers
Made by VITRA
www.vitra.com

Josef Albers was mainly involved in furniture design during his time at the Bauhaus in Weimar, where, for a short time, he was also artistic director of the furniture workshop. Vitra Design Museum has re-issued his Nesting Tables- originally created for the so-called Moellenhof House in Berlin (1926-27)- they combine clear geometrical shapes with use of colour derived from Albers' painterly oeuvre. On the under side, the glass table tops are lacquered turquoise, yellow, red, or blue. Collection Vitra Design Museum.

Josef Albers se dedicó al diseño de mobiliario principalmente durante su estancia en la Bauhaus de Weimar, donde también fue director artístico del taller de muebles durante un breve período. Las mesas auxiliares reeditadas por el Vitra Design Museum - diseñadas originariamente para la casa de los Moellenhof en Berlín (1926-27)- combinan formas geométricas claras con el empleo magistral del color, derivado de la obra pictórica de Albers. La cara inferior de los tableros de cristal está barnizada en turquesa, amarillo, rojo o azul. Colección Vitra Design Museum.

DOMUS
Designed by B&B Italia
Made by B&B ITALIA
www.bebitalia.it

Articulated in a number of configurations, DOMUS is a very complex system, which provided containers closed by doors with metallic supports and tops, bookcases with sliding doors, open elements, drawers and base-boards studied to connect all the other elements. An innovative role within the system is represented by the most recent models, born from combining the wall-mounted boiserie element together with a 70 cm. deep overhanging shelf. There are two important compositions: the first one providing a solution as bookcase or tv set holder. The second one creates a very well equipped work area.

DOMUS es un sistema muy complejo a base de contenedores cerrados por puertas con estructuras metálicas, librerías con puertas corredizas, elementos abiertos, cajones y rodapiés muy estudiados para unir todos los elementos entre si. Ideal para usar como librería o colocar la televisión, también puede utilizarse como una completa zona de trabajo.

DOUBLE DECKER DINING
& DOUBLE DECKER COFFE
Designed by Marcel Wanders
Made by MOOOI
www.moooi.nl

The table top consists of two separate layers.
Colours: natural oil, natural lacquer, white wash, grey brown, wenge, bloody brown, black.
Material: American solid oak, stained and lacquered in 7 different colours (stains with visible wood structure).

Moooi nos presenta estas dos mesas para el salón. El tablero consiste en dos capas separadas.
Colores: petróleo natural, lacado natural, blanco lavado, gris marrón, wenge, marrón sangre y negro.
Materiales: roble americano, lacado en siete colores diferentes (las manchas naturales de la madera quedan visibles).

LATE SOFA
Designed by Ronan & Erwan Bouroullec
Made by VITRA
www.vitra.com

LATE SOFA is a multi-functional sofa for relaxing, reading, watching TV or even working. Flexible, fabric or leather-covered panels create, as it were, a protective basket, in which soft seat and back cushioning provides a high degree of comfort. Attachable luminaires, trays and arm rests mean Late Sofa can be adapted to suit the user's every wish. (Trays and luminaire holder available as of July 1st, 2006).

El LATE SOFA es un sofá multifuncional para relajarse, leer, ver la televisión o para trabajar. Los paneles flexibles tapizados en tela o cuero forman en cierto modo una cesta protectora en la que los cojines blandos en el asiento y el respaldo ofrecen un gran confort. El Late Sofa, que se puede ampliar con lámparas, baldas de almacenamiento o cojines para los reposabrazos, se puede definir de forma variable según los deseos del usuario. (Las baldas y los soportes para lámparas estarán disponibles a partir de julio de 2006).

COFFEE TABLE
Designed by Isamu Noguchi
Made by VITRA
www.vitra.com

Noguchi himself described Coffee Table as his best furniture design, no doubt because it is extremely reminiscent of his bronze and marble sculptures of the time, translating the latter's biomorphic formal language unadulterated into a piece of sculptural furniture: glass tabletop resting on two identical wooden elements placed at right angles. Collection Vitra Design Museum, © The Isamu Noguchi Foundation.

El propio Noguchi calificó su Coffee Table como su mejor diseño de mueble, quizá porque le recuerda mucho a sus antiguas esculturas de bronce y mármol y porque su forma natural la convierte en un auténtico mueble escultórico: sobre dos elementos idénticos de madera en ángulo recto descansa un pesado tablero de cristal con un grosor. Colección Vitra Design Museum, © The Isamu Noguchi Foundation.

PILASTRO TABLE
Designed by Enzo Mari
Made by MAGIS
www.magisdesign.com

Table designed by Enzo Mari for Magis. Legs made with polished die-cast aluminium. Top in MDF veneered in oak or in HPL with laminate cover white and edge in polished aluminium.

Mesa diseñada por Enzo Mari para Magis. Las patas han sido fabricadas con aluminio pulido y el tablero en MDF chapado con roble en HPL cubierto por aluminio blanco pulido.

CENTOMILA POLTRONCINA
Designed by James Irvine
Made by VITRA
www.vitra.com

Stacking low chair. Also available with arms. Materials: frame in steel tube painted in epoxy resin or chromed. Seat, back and top in standard injection-moulded polypropylene.

Silla apilable. Disponible también con brazos. Materiales: estructura de acero pintado con resina o cromado. El asiento y el respaldo han sido fabricados con polipropileno por inyección.

IPE CAVALLI
Designed by Ipe Cavalli
Made by IPE CAVALLI
www.ipe-cavalli.com

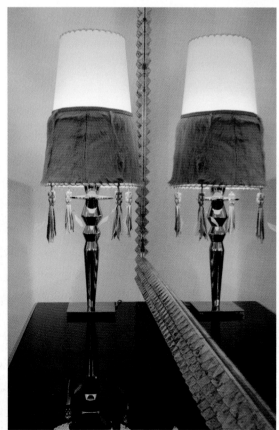

IPE CAVALLI
Designed by Ipe Cavalli
Made by IPE CAVALLI
www.ipe-cavalli.com

Neo Gothic design and contemporary-basic blend together to create a combination of Fashion, absolute Glamorous. Reflective surfaces of glass retro-lacquered, finished with chromed steel, soft velvets and suede leathers are easily confused to the touch. Fabrics and sheen which recall antique clothing, armour of nobles and medieval knights.
The combination of rigour and opulence is forseen even for the large table in steel and lacquered glass combined with soft embracing chairs in the "dining room", illuminated by unique ceiling lamps produced exclusively by Italamp for the Visionnaire Collection.

Diseño Neo Gótico y comtemporáneo se mezclan para crear una combinación muy moderna, absolutamente glamurosa. Superficies reflectantes de cristal retro-lacado, acabados con acero cromado, terciopelo suave y ante de cuero son fácilmente confundibles al tacto. Los tejidos y el brillo nos recuerdan a la ropa antigua, nos transporta a las armaduras de los nobles caballeros medievales.
La combinación de rigor y opulencia se refleja hasta en la gran mesa que han diseñado para el salón con cristal y acero lacadao, iluminado por lámparas de techo únicas producidas exclusivamente por Italamp para la colección Visionnaire.

TAÒ EXTENDABLE TABLE
Designed by Dondoli & Pocci
Made by BONALDO
www.bonaldo.it

The extendable table TAÒ is a refined and elegant table. Clean and essential lines with a geometric and linear shape, TAÒ is a table equipped with an extension that opens like a book.
The structure is in chrome-plated metal; the top is in crystal, while the extension is in laminate, both of them available in black and white.

TAÒ es una refinada y elegante mesa extensible. De líneas puras y limpias con una forma geométrica y lineal, TAÒ es una mesa equipada con un ala extensible que se abre como un libro.
La estructura se ha realizado en metal cromado plateado, la mesa es de cristal, mientras que la extensión está hecha en laminado, ambos están disponibles en blanco y en negro.

SURFER TABLE
Designed by Giuseppe Viganò
Made by BONALDO
www.bonaldo.it

SURFER is a large oval or round table designed for elegant living or dining rooms. The imposing base in chrome-plated or varnished steel in the shape of a cross contrasts with the lightness of the top in serigraphed crystal in white, black or Parapan® (a particular technical material with a polished, mirror-like finish).

SURFER es una mesa ovalada o redonda diseñada para comedores o salones muy elegantes. La imponente base de metal varnizado, o cromado, en forma de cruz contrasta con la ligereza del cristal serigrafiado en blanco, negro o Parapan® (un particular material con un acabado de espejo).

ELLE COLLECTION
Designed by Domodinamica
Made by DOMODINAMICA
www.domodinamica.com

These beautiful chairs made by Domodinamica are
realized in polyurethane resins cold foamed in die and
supported by a base in drawn wire steel chromed
covered with fabrics or leathers.

Estas preciosas sillas fabricadas por Domodinamica
han sido realizadas con espuma de resinas de poliuretano sobre una estructura base de acero cromado
forradas con telas o cuero.

MIST TABLE
Designed by Rodrigo Torres
Made by DOMODINAMICA
www.domodinamica.com

MIST table designed by fabulous designer Rodrigo Torres is one of the best products of Domodinamica, with its organic lines is the perfect table for the most modern customers. The structure in steel pipe chromed is assembled by shell mold casting joints in aluminium brushed and chromed. The top in tempered crystal recall steel colour.

La mesa MIST diseñada por Rodrigo Torres es una de los mejores productos de Domodinamica, de lineas casi orgánicas, es la mesa perfecta para los más modernos. La estructura es de tubo de acero cromado. Se cepillan y pulen las uniones para que de el resultado final sea el de una sola pieza. El cristal de la mesa ha sido templado para lograr un efecto que nos recuerda al acero.

NEXTMARUNI CHAIR
Designed by Azumi
Made by AZUMI
www.azumi.co.uk

This is a chair which looks paper thin, but it has an upholstered seat and back padding within the wooden frame. This design applied the technology of 3D wood curving by CNC router, and highly skilled craftsmanship of upholstery which Maruni developed in their history. Collaborated with Tomoko Azumi.

Esta silla parece fina como el papel, pero tiene una resistente estructura de madera sobre la que descansan el asiento y el respaldo. Para realizar este diseño Azumi aplicó la técnologia 3D que retuerce la madera por CNC, una técnica que Maruni desarrolló en el campo de la tapicería. Colaboración con Tomoko Azumi.

GUÉRIDON BAS
Designed by Jean Prouvé
Made by VITRA
www.vitra.com

In the early 1940s Jean Prouvé turned his attention increasingly to wood as a material. In the case of the Guéridon Bas coffee table a sturdy top is positioned on three solid oak feet. The elements are connected to each other by means of a folded sheet metal construction. Referencing a tropical wood version of the time entitled "Table Africaine", this re-edition is also available in impregnated dark oak.

Esta silla, desarrollada a principios de los años cincuenta para la Cité Universitaire de Antony, en París, representa uno de los últimos trabajos de Prouvé en el ámbito del diseño de mobiliario. El poder de seducción de este exclusivo asiento radica en su diseño poco convencional que Prouvé supo unir a una forma sorprendente y dinámica.

Bedtime stories

descansa con diseño

A dream paradise does exist. This private and protective sanctuary away from the trials of life is to be found in a corner of the house.
From the intimate depths of our minds we travel rapidly, projecting future desires at the same time playing witness to the day's outcome.
The living manifestation of this area is, without doubt, a transcendental and creative task into which the designers have put all their ingenuity to create the designs which are brought to you in this chapter in an all-embracing collection of images which form the basis of this task, visually furnishing the mind with suggestions which are attuned to our personality and drive us on to create a pleasant receptacle for our dreams.

El paraíso de los sueños existe. Está en un rincón de la casa, refugio privado y protector del desafío vital.
Desde su intimidad, nuestra mente viaja rápidamente proyectando deseos futuros, y recordando el devenir del día.
La materialización de este espacio, es sin duda una tarea trascendental y creativa, en la que los diseñadores han puesto su mayor carga de ingenio para desarrollar los diseños que, en este capítulo les presentamos con un amplio repertorio de imágenes que, vertebra el corpus de la obra alimentando la mirada con sugerencias que, afines a nuestra personalidad nos empuje a inventar un receptáculo cordial para nuestros sueños.

On the following pages furniture by Bonaldo.
En las páginas siguientes mobiliario de Bonaldo.

PAD DOUBLE BED
Designed by Giuseppe Viganò
Made by BONALDO
www.bonaldo.it

PAD has a table, available with different oak finishes, that is mounted on large wheels and can be moved in several directions thanks to a track hidden in the lateral frame of the bed. As with all Bonaldo beds, in Pad too, the base that supports the mattress can be regulated in height and the frame is available in different sizes.

El modelo PAD tiene una mesita de noche, disponible en distintos acabados en roble, montada sobre unas grandes ruedas que se mueven en distintas direcciones gracias a un raíl escondido en el lateral de la cama. Como en todas las camas de Bonaldo, se puede regular la altura de la base que soporta el somier y el colchón.

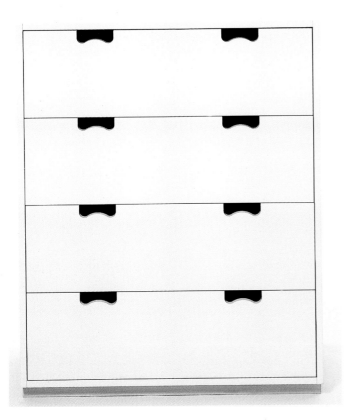

CABINET A
Designed by Jonas Bohlin & Thomas Sandell
Made by ASPLUND

www.asplund.org

The Asplund Collection is a collection of modern high-quality products with roots in Swedish tradition and handicraft. The essence of the collection is functional, clean shaped, and elegant products with a Swedish-internatinoal feel. CABINET A is a storage cabinet for various enviroments: for both home and office.

La Colección Asplund es una colección de productos de alta calidad muy modernos con raíces de la artesanía tradicional Sueca. La esencia de la colección es la funcionalidad, de líneas pura, y productos elegantes con un toque internacional.
El CABINET A es un armario con cajones perfecto tanto para interiores domésticos como para la oficina.

CABINET C
Designed by Jonas Bohlin & Thomas Sandell
Made by ASPLUND
www.asplund.org

By the hand of Jonas Bohlin and Thomas Sandell comes the beautiful CABINET C also from the Asplund collection with the same concept and ellegance.

De la mano de los diseñadores Jonas Bohlin y Thomas Sandell, el CABINET C mantiene ell mismo concepto y elegancia de la Colección Asplund.

101

BREST
Designed by G. Cappellini
Made by CAPPELLINI
www.cappellini.it

Collection of units with doors and drawers, available macroter or polish lacquered in the colours of the collection, in natural or ash-grey stained oak and in natural santos. Varniched steel bases, aluminium or dark-grey colours, anodized aluminium or dark-grey varnished handles. To complete the collection are also available mirrors in two different heights to be used on units, in natural, smoke-grey or blue finish with anodized or dark-grey varnished aluminium frame.

Capellini nos presenta esta elegante pero moderna colección de muebles para el dormitorio con puertas y cajones en distintos acabados y colores de alta calidad. Complementamos la colección con unos espejos en dos alturas distintas también con distintos acabados en el cristal.

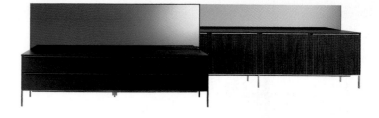

BALIOS
Designed by Axo light
Made by AXO LIGHT
www.axolight.it

Glass curves, light that expands the environment and blurs the outlines. Crystal wings that seem bent on the desire for light to come forward, sweeping away all it finds in its path. Ongoing recalls of light and shade, veils and tears that move the scene, accurately studied areas of light and shade to create a background for intriguing and sophisticated atmospheres. Rigor and minimalism but also emotions for a collection of glass lamps that become a natural component in both public and private contemporary spaces thanks to their versatility. In fact, the light filtered through a particular curve or the natural transparency of glass, lends the environment warmth and a sense of wellbeing.
Balios is offered in the wall and hanging versions, in the colors white, coffee and chrome. The finishes are in chrome-plated metal.

Curvas de vidrio, luz que dilata los ambientes y que difumina sus contornos. Alas de cristal que parecen rendidas al deseo de la luz de abrirse un camino arrollando todo lo que encuentra. Referencias continuas de claroscuros, ofuscaciones y aberturas que mueven la escena, áreas de luz y de sombra estudiadas con precisión para hacer de fondo a atmósferas intrigantes y sofisticadas. Rigor y minimalismo pero también emoción para una colección de lámparas de vidrio que por su versatilidad se incorpora naturalmente en espacios contemporáneos tanto públicos como privados. En efecto, la luz filtrada por la curvatura particular y por la transparencia natural del vidrio, aporta a los ambientes calor y sensación de bienestar.
Balios se propone en las aplicaciones de pared y de suspensión, con los colores blanco, café y cromo. Los acabados son de metal cromado.

WHITE ACRYLIC DRAWER UNIT
Designed by Paul Kelley
Made by PAUL KELLEY
www.pk-designs.co.uk

Paul Kelley has designed this amazing acrylic outer shell with Polyrey buffalo skin laminate drawers.
Measurements:
2000mm X 560mm X 500mm.

Paul Kelley ha diseñado este maravilloso mueble para la habitación de matrimonio en acrílico con cajones de piel de buffalo laminado.
Medidas:
2000mm X 560mm X 500mm.

ALUMINIUM AND ACRYLIC UNIT
Designed by Paul Kelley
Made by PAUL KELLEY
www.pk-designs.co.uk

Aluminium section is finished in solid aluminium sheet on the exterior and black gloss laminate on the interior. All door and cabinet edges are mitred and lipped in solid walnut. Orange section lifts up to reveal drinks bar detailed in solid walnut. End section is made entirely from 18 mm solid black acrylic with the 3 drawers being lined in black laminate.
3500mm X 900mm X 500mm.

Sección de aluminio terminada con láminas de aluminio sólido en el exterior y laminado negro brillante en su interior. Todas las puertas, bordes y esquinas son de madera de nogal. La sección de color naranja que se eleva nos revela un práctico mueble bar también con detalles en nogal. La sección final está hecha enteramente con acrílico de 18 mm y los 3 cajones han sido realizados en laminado de color negro.
3500mm X 900mm X 500mm.

KALM
Designed by Karim Rashid
Made by BONALDO
www.karimrashid.com
www.bonaldo.it

The double bed KALM, with its slender and minimal shape with the headboard that surrounds it almost embracing the structure and the mattress, offers a sense of calm and relaxation. This peculiar "embrace" consists of a metal, leather-covered structure with contrast stitching, that can function as a small shelf for a book or an alarm clock. The metal feet in a peculiar "V" shape help make Kalm's line light and slender.

KALM es la cama de matrimonio diseñada por Karim Rashid para Bonaldo. Destacamos la cabecera que rodea con un "abrazo" toda la estructura y el colchón aportando calma y relajación. Este peculiar "abrazo" consiste en una estructura metálica, cubierta por cuero con las costuras visibles, hace las veces de estantería en la que apoyar un libro o un despertador. Los pies en forma de "V" siguen la línea suave y minimalista de este diseño exquisito.

NIGHT
Designed by Carlo Colombo
Made by ZANOTTA
www.zanotta.it

Bed with or without container unit. Base in nickel-plated and brushed steel or varnished graphite. Varnished steel frame. Springing in natural bent beech strips with stiffness adjusters. Upholstered base and headboard in polyurethane/Dacron Du Pont. Removable cover in fabric or leather.

Cama con o sin canapé. La base es de niquel plateado, acero o grafito varnizado. La estructura está fabricada en acero muy resistente y el conjunto de base y cabecera han sido tapizados en poliuretano/Dracon Du Pont. La funda extraíble se puede encontrar en tela o en cuero.

ESU
Designed by Charles & Ray Eames
Made by VITRA
www.vitra.com

Charles and Ray Eames developed a new system of free-standing multifunctional shelves which - similar to the Eames House that dates from the same time - were constructed strictly in keeping with the principles of industrial mass production: the Eames Storage Units (ESU).

Charles & Ray Eames desarrollaron un novedoso sistema de estanterías multifuncionales, las Eames Storage Units (ESU), construidas siguiendo los principios de la producción industrial en serie - al igual que la Eames House, construida al mismo tiempo.

OSCAR
Designed by Emaf Progetti
Made by ZANOTTA
www.zanotta.it

Night table with drawer. Steel frame, chromium-plated or varnished graphite or aluminium. Handle in glossy anodised aluminium or painted graphite or aluminium. Drawer in medium density fiberboard veneered in assembled sliced veneer Ebony, natural matt or with bleached oak, wengé-stained or varnished grey, white or red.

Mesita de noche con cajón. Marco de acero, cromado plateado o grafito varnizado o aluminio. Perfecto para las habitaciones de matrimonio de carácter más minimalista.

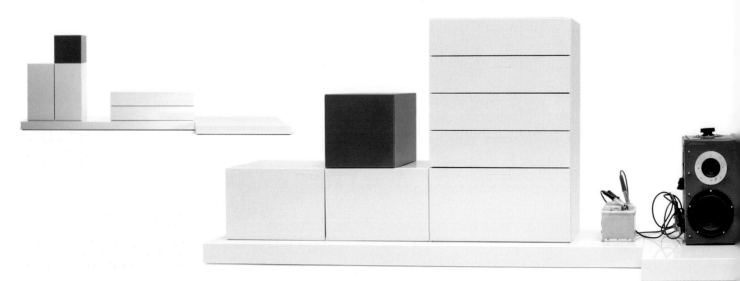

CITY SYSTEM
Designed Marcel Wanders
Made by MOOOI
www.moooi.com

Our particular city landscape in the bedroom made of units with doors and drawers in white with some red hints.

Nuestra pequeña ciudad dentro del dormitorio hecha de armarios con puertas y cajones de color blanco con algún pequeño toque en rojo.

THE KEBAB LAMP
Designed by Committe
Made by COMMITTE
www.gallop.co.uk

The Committee KEBAB LAMP stands are made by skewering a collection of found objects, antiques and other miscellany no longer in use with the aim of delighting the viewer with an explosion of colour and reference. Built as a totem of improbably varied materials, the lamps are carefully composed to contain stories and meanings amongst the eclectic objects they include and consequently each lamp is unique and filled with pieces from different eras that allude to the constant turning of fashion and style.

The concept behind the lamps was born of Committee's interest in the way people relate to and value objects and the lamps play with this sense of value as fine porcelain and plastic come together to form a sculptural composition with its own integrity. The lamps are also intended to be explorations of 'taste', whilst simultaneously referring to the consumption of material goods and the inevitable waste this produces. Of course they can also light your room...

Committee is very pleased to add that the lamps won the UK Elle Decoration/Observer Design Award for Best in Lighting 2004. In 2005 they were selected to appear in the German Design Council's "Interior Innovations Award" at Cologne after which a collection of lamps was presented at Dilmos design gallery for the Milan Furniture Fair 05 and at Cibone design store for Tokyo Design Week 05.

Las lámparas KEBAB de Committee han sido diseñadas a partir de una colección de objetos reciclados, algunos encontrados en anticuarios y otros en la basura, con el ánimo de provocar en el espectardor una explosión de color y recuerdos del pasado. Construídas como una especie "totems", las lámparas contienen historias, nos transmiten mensajes y nos provocan sensaciones, atacan directamente a nuestros recuerdos. Cada lámpara es única, no existen dos iguales, llenas de piezas de diferentes eras que aluden al constante cambio de la moda y el diseño.

El concepto de estas lámparas nació del interés de Committee por la manera en la que las personas valoran sus objetos personales, las lámparas juegan con esta sensación de valor: porcelna fina y plástico se juntan para formar una composición escultórica con su propia integridad. Las lámparas intentan explorar el "buen gusto" y por supuesto su función es la de iluminar...

Comittee ha ganado varios galardones durante los últimos años como el UK Elle Decoration/Observer Design Award a la mejor Iluminación 2004. En el año 2005 fueron seleccionados para el German Design Council's "Interior Innovations Award" en Colonia, despues de que su colección de lámparas fuera presentada en la galería Dilmos durante la feria del mueble de Milán y en la tienda Cibon Design durante la semana del diseño en Tokio.

111

BOX
Designed by Emaf Progetti
Made by ZANOTTA
www.zanotta.it

Bed with container unit. Base in nickel-plated and brushed steel or varnished graphite. Varnished steel frame. Springing in natural bent beech strips with stiffness adjusters. Upholstered base and headboard in polyurethane/Dacron Du Pont. Removable cover in fabric or leather.

La base de esta cama es de niquel plateado, acero o grafito varnizado. La estructura está fabricada en acero muy resistente y el conjunto de base y cabecera han sido tapizados en poliuretano/Dracon Du Pont. La funda extraíble se puede encontrar en tela o en cuero. Este modelo ademas incluye canapé muy útil para liberar espacio de los armarios.

BLOW
Designed by Wok Media
Made by WOK
www.wokmedia.com

A ball shaped fan switched on and off using a baby fan mounted on its casing. You blow the little fan to turn on the main propeller, then stop it with your finger to switch it off. The fans spherical mesh body sits in a coil of cable like an egg in an egg cup so that it can be angled exactly as you need it. Your interaction with Blow is both playful and threatening, the tension around the normally forbidden action of putting your finger in a fan is set against the delightful discovery that your blow is answered in the same language.

BLOW es un pequeño y original ventilador, perfecto para colocar en la mesita de noche. La particularidad de este ventilador, aparte de su diseño en forma de nido, es la interacción entre el objeto y su propietario, ya que podemos encendero y apagarlo con tan sólo un dedo.

FALL IN LOVE
Designed by Axo Light
Made by AXO LIGHT
www.axolight.com

Labyrinths of light and color, magical expressions that play with bright color contrasts. Shapes, colors and materials mingle in total creative liberty; pure exaltation of the great potential for emotional and expressive impact that is natural to light. Emotional and vital, the FALL IN LOVE collection is a real concentrate of energy thanks to the colors and the new materials that conquer you instinctively. This kind of design expresses a desire for experimentation that goes beyond production demands. It is a meticulous and precise investigation of the use, function and shape of objects of everyday life that has the objective of reinterpreting and reinventing them without neglecting the functional needs of the object. The FALL IN LOVE collection is in two-color (white and yellow) metacrylate with great light diffusing power and it comes in hanging and table lamp versions.

Laberintos de luz y de color, expresiones mágicas que juegan con la luz y el contraste del color. Formas, colores y materiales se mezclan en total armonía y libertad; pura exaltación del gran potencial a nivel emocional y expresivo del impacto natural de la luz. Emocional y vital, la colección FALL IN LOVE es un concetrado de energía gracias a los colores y los nuevos materiales que te conquistan instantáneamente. Este tipo de diseño expresa un deseo por la experimentación que va más allá de su producción en serie. Detrás hay una profunda investigación del uso, función y forma de los objetos que usamos en el día a día, con el objetivo de reinventar o reinterpretar el concepto pero sin restar la funcionalidad que se necesita en cada objeto. La colección FALL IN LOVE se ha fabricado en dos colores (blanco y amarillo) de metacrilato con un gran poder difusor de la luz y en sus dos versiones, una para colgar y otra para sobremesa.

METAL SIDE TABLES
Designed by Ronan & Erwan Bouroullec
Made by VITRA
www.vitra.com

The METAL SIDE TABLES belong to that category of furniture, which, while not being the focal point of the fittings, is nonetheless indispensable in making them complete. Small, rather unassuming aids, they can be easily moved to other locations and used for a wide variety of purposes, performing a wide range of valuable services. Thanks to the harmony of their dimensions and the attractive formal contrast between slender table tops and voluminous, socle-like legs, they make an attractive addition wherever they stand.

Las METAL SIDE TABLES pertenecen a una categoría de muebles que, sin ser elementos esenciales del equipamiento, resultan indispensables para completarlo. Así, se trata de pequeños ayudantes, más bien discretos, que desempeñan todo tipo de valiosos servicios, pueden cambiar de lugar con facilidad y se pueden utilizar para los fines más diversos. Gracias a sus armónicas proporciones y al sugestivo contraste de formas entre los tableros delgados y las voluminosas patas, diseñadas en forma de zócalo, estos muebles auxiliares presentan una bonita figura en cualquier lugar.

EAK DRESSER
Designed by Piet Hein Eek
Made by MOOOI
www.moooi.nl

The beautifully-rich baroque dresser from Piet Hein Eek boast all the charismatic delights of Moooi, with clean lines and noted craftsmanship.

Piet Hein es el diseñador responsable de los preciosos estampados barrocos de casi todos los productos de Moooi, con líneas limpias y acabados artesanales.

COPPER AND ACRYLIC TALLBOY
Designed by Paul Kelley
Made by PAUL KELLEY
www.pk-designs.co.uk

18 Gauge copper sheet exterior solid acrylic interior with solid walnut drawers on concealed runners adjustable feet.
Dimensions:
1800 X 550 X 500 mm

El exterior de esta precioso mueble es de cobre, mientras que los interiores son de acrílico sólido y los cajones de nuez que han diseñado con raíles ocultos. Las patas, en la base, son ajustables.
Dimensiones:
1800 X 550 X 500 mm

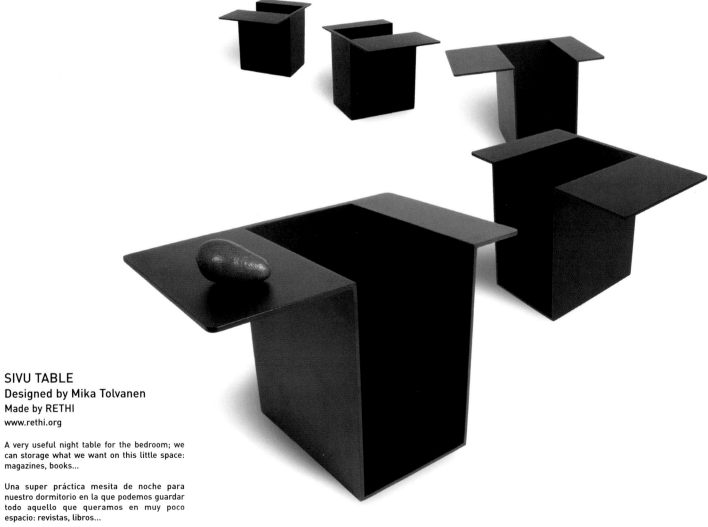

SIVU TABLE
Designed by Mika Tolvanen
Made by RETHI
www.rethi.org

A very useful night table for the bedroom; we can storage what we want on this little space: magazines, books...

Una super práctica mesita de noche para nuestro dormitorio en la que podemos guardar todo aquello que queramos en muy poco espacio: revistas, libros...

KEPLERO
Designed by Axo light
Made by AXO LIGHT
www.axolight.it

Further diffusers placed above and below, light up the upper and lower parts of the room creating a warm and rarified atmosphere. KEPLERO is available as a floor, table, hanging and wall lamp.

En la parte superior e inferior de la lámpara, ulteriores difusores permiten la iluminación de la habitación hacia arriba y hacia abajo creando una atmósfera cálida y enrarecida. KEPLERO se encuentra disponible como lámpara de pie, de mesa, suspendida y de pared.

CABINET B
Designed by Jonas Bohlin & Thomas Sandell
Made by ASPLUND
www.asplund.org

The Asplund Collection is a collection of modern high-quality products with roots in Swedish tradition and handicraft. The essence of the collection is functional, clean shaped, and elegant products with a Swedish-internatinoal feel. CABINET B is a storage cabinet for various enviroments: for both home and office.

La Colección Asplund es una colección de productos de alta calidad muy modernos con raíces de la artesanía tradicional Sueca. La esencia de la colección es la funcionalidad, de líneas pura, y productos elegantes con un toque internacional. El CABINET B es un armario con cajones perfecto tanto para interiores domésticos como para la oficina.

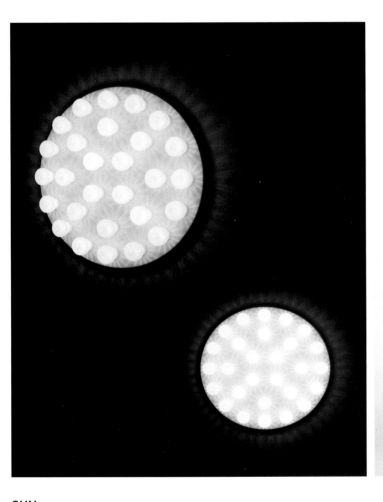

SUN
Designed by Tonylight
Made by SPHAUS
www.sphaus.com

Ceiling or wall light. The base is matt white powder-coated steel. Bulbs are protected by an opalescent methylacrylate cover that gives the light a golden hue and creates a curious star-like effect.

Lámpara de pared o techo. La base es de acero mate pintado en color blanco. Las bombillas quedan protegidas por un plafón de metacrilato opalescente que le da a la luz un toque dorado, creando una curiosa sensación de luz de estrellas.

IPE CAVALLI
Designed by Ipe Cavalli
Made by IPE CAVALLI
www.ipe-cavalli.com

Neo Gothic design and contemporary-basic blend together to create a combination of Fashion, absolute Glamorous. Reflective surfaces of glass retro-lacquered, finished with chromed steel, soft velvets and suede leathers are easily confused to the touch. Fabrics and sheen which recall antique clothing, armour of nobles and medieval knights.
The combination of rigour and opulence is forseen even for the large table in steel and lacquered glass combined with soft embracing chairs in the "dining room", illuminated by unique ceiling lamps produced exclusively by Italamp for the Visionnaire Collection.

Diseño Neo Gótico y comtemporáneo se mezclan para crear una combinación muy moderna, absolutamente glamurosa. Superficies reflectantes de cristal retro-lacado, acabados con acero cromado, terciopelo suave y ante de cuero son fácilmente confundibles al tacto. Los tejidos y el brillo nos recuerdan a la ropa antigua, nos transporta a las armaduras de los nobles caballeros medievales.
La combinación de rigor y opulencia se refleja hasta en la gran mesa que han diseñado para el salón con cristal y acero lacado, iluminado por lámparas de techo únicas producidas exclusivamente por Italamp para la colección Visionnaire.

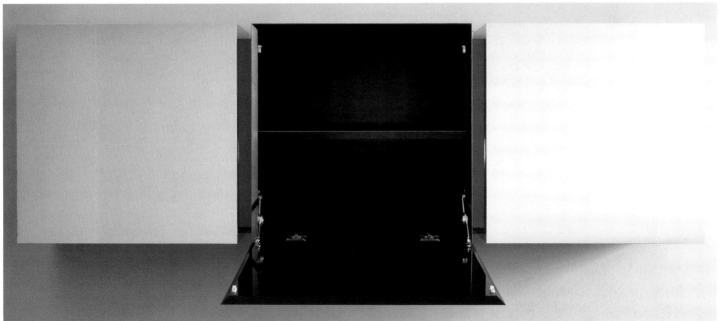

POLISHED BRASS WALL HUNG UNIT
Designed by Paul Kelley
Made by PAUL KELLEY
www.pk-designs.co.uk

Exterior finished in solid brass sheet with interior laminated in cocowood. All door and cabinet edges are mitred and lipped in solid walnut.
Measurements are 2350mm X 750mm X 350mm.

El exterior se terminó con hoja de cobre sólida con los interiores laminados en madera de coco. Todos los bordes se han terminado con madera de nogal de alta calidad.
Las medidas son 2350mm X 750mm X 350mm.

KOSHI
Designed by Axo light
Made by AXO LIGHT
www.axolight.it

The harmony of KOSHI is the result of many contrasts of shapes,
colors and materials. The opalescence of blown glass, the glittering
reflections of metal, the strong nuances of wood give life to an
intriguing play of shades, a sophisticated combination of materials
and expert workmanship. The collection is available in hanging,
table, floor, wall and ceiling versions in different sizes

La armonía de KOSHI se apoya en un espeso contraste de formas, de
colores y de materiales. La opalescencia del vidrio soplado, los
reflejos chispeantes del metal, los matices decididos de la madera
dan vida a un intrigante juego de sombras, un sofisticado connubio
de materiales y de sabios trabajos. La colección se encuentra
disponible en las aplicaciones suspendida, de mesa, de pie, de pared
y de techo en diversos tamaños.

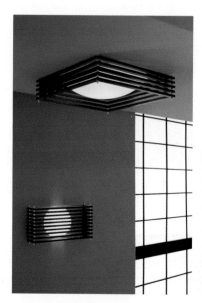

CLAVIUS
Designed by Axo light
Made by AXO LIGHT
www.axolight.it

CLAVIUS, the collection of lamps with a chrome frame and a shade worked by hand with thin silken threads, expresses and exalts the profound relationship between light, matter, shape and color to create examples of lighting magic. The CLAVIUS collection is available in ivory white and tobacco. The frame is chrome- plated and the diffuser in opaline metacrylate.

El diseño esencial, refinado en su linealidad, crea un juego de luces y sombras, un alternar-se de tonalidades cromáticas y de reflejos que la trama del difusor contrasta con maestría, regalando atmósferas llenas de encanto y estilo en todos los ambientes. La montura es cromada y el difusor es de metacrilato opalino. La colección está compuesta por la versión suspendida, de tierra, de pared y de techo en diversos tamaños.

Play, fun and sweet dreams!

¡juega, diviértete y dulces sueños!

The perception and the mind of a child are like a blank tape, an empty box continuously being filled with everything the child sees and feels each day. Touch and vision are the two senses and primary tools with which the child embarks upon its journey through the world during the first few years of its existence.

These early experiences are filled with the warmth of the hearth, when the senses are permanently receptive to every detail and every nook and cranny remains firmly embedded in the child's mind to be later dissected and recreated.

The aim of the following pages is to be an exponent of those designs which currently synthesise these infantile worlds in which reality makes sense, portrayed as it is in these ingenious designs.

La mirada y la mente del niño son como cintas en blanco, como un cajón vacío que se va llenando con todo lo que éste ve y siente cada día. El tacto y la vista son sus dos herramientas básicas para viajar por el mundo durante los primeros años de su existencia.

El calor del hogar llena esas primeras experiencias, cuando los sentidos están permanentemente desplegados y cada detalle, cada rincón, queda grabado en la mente infantil para ser diseccionado y recreado.

Las siguientes páginas pretenden ser un exponente de los diseños que en la actualidad sintetizan estos ambientes infantiles, mostrando en ese orden de ideas, ingeniosos diseños donde la realidad cobra sentido.

On the following pages furniture by Mi Cuna.
En las páginas siguientes mobiliario de Mi Cuna.

ORBITAL WORKSTATION
Designed by Azumi Tomoko
Made by AZUMI
www.azumi.co.uk

Supported by Design Council and Department for the Education and Skills of the UK, this piece of furniture is designed for secondary schools. The chair orbit around the centre pole of the round table, and it allows students to face teacher and change directions in smooth action. It has gas lift height adjustment, weight locking castors, as well as hook for their bags, which can be used for a handle when it is wheeled around.
Seat & Desk top: Plywood.
Structure: Powder coated steel.
W=1450 D=700 H=700 mm

Patrocinado por el Design Council y el Departamento para la Educación y Técnicas del Reino Unido, esta pieza de mobiliario está diseñanda para los alumnos de secundaria. La silla orbita alrededor de la mesa, y permite a los alumnos moverse de una manera suave y silenciosa. La altura se regula mediante gas y tiene un colgador para las carteras. Un mueble super útil también en casa, no ocupa mucho lugar y sirve como escritorio para hacer los deberes además de ser muy decorativo.
Asiento y tabla: Contrachapado.
Estructura: Acero.
W=1450 D=700 H=700 mm

MONO
Designed by René Hougaard & Jens Hombak
Made by DNMARK
www.dnmark.com

One table, one colour. Mono is a simple and functional table lacquered in one colour. The table can be delivered in a long range of colours, to suit all types of interior.

Una mesa, un color. Mono es una simple y funcional mesa laqueada en un solo color. Está disponible en un amplio abanico de colores para que se ajuste a cualquier tipo de interiores.

GUÉRIDON
Designed by Jean Prouvé
Made by VITRA
www.vitra.com

Prouvé designed the Guéridon Table, with its particularly impressive structural clarity, for the University of Paris. This wooden table proves that modern tables do not have to be made of steel and glass and offers a variation on Prouvé's standard formal language, with its architectural overtones, by using a natural material.

Prouvé diseñó la mesa Guéridon para la Universidad de París, donde sorprendió principalmente por su claridad constructiva. Esta mesa de madera demuestra que las mesas modernas no deben ser necesariamente de acero y cristal y supone un cambio en el lenguaje formal de Prouvé, marcadamente arquitectónico, al emplear un material natural.

STANDARD CHAIR
Designed by Jean Prouvé
Made by VITRA
www.vitra.com

Chairs take the most strain on their back legs, where they bear the weight of their user's upper body. Prouvé took this into account very succinctly in Standard Chair. Tubular steel piping is enough for the front legs that take relatively little strain, whereas the back legs are made of voluminous hollow sections and pass the strain on to the floor.

La carga de una silla es mayor en sus patas traseras, donde debe absorber el peso de la parte superior del cuerpo. Prouvé aplicó este sencillo principio en la Standard Chair de manera significativa. Mientras que para las patas delanteras, con una carga relativamente débil, basta con un tubo de acero, las patas traseras se han diseñado como un cuerpo hueco voluminoso que transmite la carga al suelo.

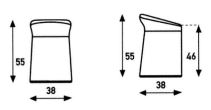

LILLA
Designed by Patrick Norguet
Made by ARTIFORT
www.artifort.com

An invitation to sit down, reduced to the most simple expression like a tree-trunk in a residential environment or where ergonomics serve the body. This object evolves in the middle of a space as a playful and simple seating element which distinguishes itself in both colour and material. Cast foam with a steel tubular frame. Designed for both the residential and the contract market. Available in various Artifort fabrics and leather materials.

Con la forma de un tronco de árbol partido este taburete invita a sentarnos. Este objeto no pasará desapercibido ya que se distingue fácilmente por su color y el material del que está fabricado: espuma de molde con un marco tubular de acero. Disponible en varios tejidos Artifort y cuero. Es ideal para las habitaciones infantiles ya que aporta un toque de color muy divertido.

GUÉRIDON
Designed by Herbert Klamminger and BKM
Made by VITRA
www.vitra.com

Gueridon es un sujeta libros, una estantería de sobremesa y un escritorio de lectura en uno. Tan práctico como decorativo nos permite tener siempre a mano y de una manera ordenada el último libro que estamos leyendo.

Gueridon is a book end, a table top bookcase and lectern all in one. Both practical and decorative it allows us to always to have the book we are currently reading conveniently to hand.

HI-POUFF
Designed by Matali Crasset
Made by DOMODINAMICA
www.domodinamica.com

The pouff realized in indeformable foam, is covered in coloured fabric proposed in collection and is provided whit handle to make more easy the moving everywhere. All pouff can be replaced on the proper "Support Mural" composed by shelves in MDF laquered in different colours. It is a "multipurpose" object, it can be used like a building game for babies.

Este divertido pouff ha sido realizado con espuma indeformable, forrado de coloridos tejidos, dispone de unas prácticas asas para poder moverlo fácilmente de un sitio a otro. Es ideal para habitaciones infantiles, para que los niños juegen cómodamente, además gracias a la estantería que completa este set podremos tener los pouff siempre recogidos y en perfecto orden.

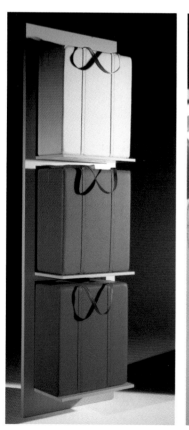

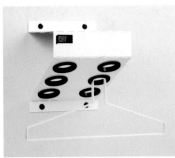
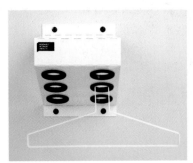
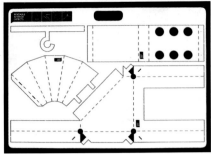

BENDABLE INTERIOR OBJECTS (BIO)
Designed by Form us with love
Made by FORM US WITH LOVE
www.formuswithloves.se

A pleasant way to make a game of children learning to tidy their own bedrooms. Actually a collection of furniture and objects designed by Form us with love. From coat hangers to stools, all are made from die-cast metal plate, highly resistant and bendable. Sure to delight even the smallest members of the household.

Una divertida manera de aprender a ordenar la habitación infantil jugando. Se trata de una colección de muebles y objetos diseñados por Form us with love. Desde un perchero hasta un taburete, realizados en láminas metálicas troqueladas muy fáciles de doblar y resitentes. Harán las delicias de los más pequeños de la casa.

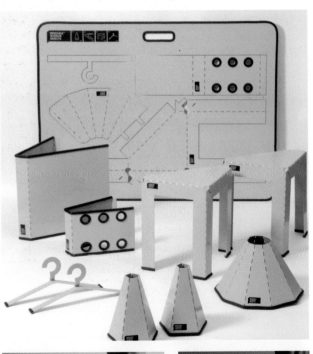

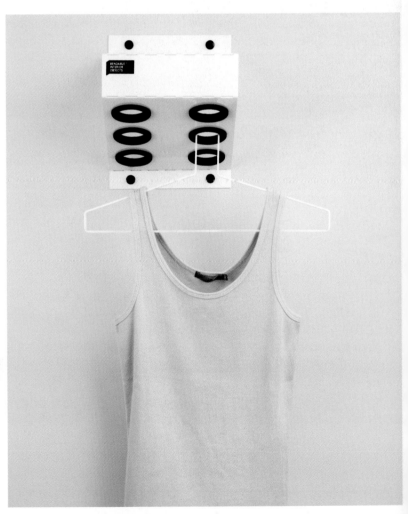

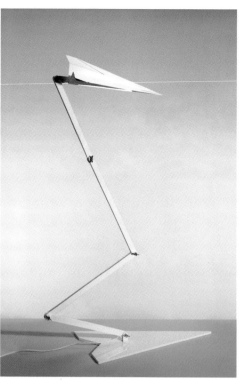
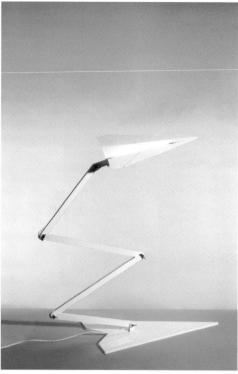

AEROPLANE LIGHT FLOOR LAMP & AEROPLANE LIGHT

Designed by Malin Lundmark
Made by MALIN LUNDMARK
www.malinlundmark.com

"Aeroplane light – floor lamp" – "Aeroplane light" with a mobile base, giving the lamp different expressions.
Material: Altered and varnished sheets of metal.
"Aeroplane light" – A pendant fluorescent lamp in the shape of a folded paper aeroplane. The simplicity of the design brings back memories of childhood play. The circuit board becomes a decorative engine on the planes exterior.
Material: Altered and varnished sheets of metal.
Size: Length 47 cm, width 25 cm.

"Aeroplane light – lampara de pie" – Se trata de la "Aeroplane light" pero con una base móvil, dándole a la lámpara diferentes expresiones.
Material: Hojas de metal barnizado.
"Aeroplane light" – Lámpara fluorescente colgante en forma de un avión de papel doblado. Un detalle simpático para la habitación de los niños.
Material: Hojas de metal barnizado.
Dimensiones: Largo 47 cm, ancho 25 cm.

JENETTE
Designed by Fernando & Humberto Campana
Made by EDRA
www.edra.com

Moulded chair made of rigid structural polyurethane, having a metallic core. Its backrest is covered of about 900 hundred flexible stalks made of rigid PVC. It is totally painted in polyurethanic opaque paints, and it is available in six colours.

Edra nos presenta esta original y divertida silla hecha de poliuretano estructural rígido, con corazón metálico. Su respaldo está cubierto por más de novecientos tallos flexibles hechos de PVC. Está pintada con pinturas de opacas de poliuretano y está disponible en llamativos colores.

AIR-TABLE
Designed by Jasper Morrison
Made by MAGIS
www.magisdesign.com

Stacking tables designed by Jasper Morrions and made by Magis with polypropylene with glass fibre added.

Mesas apilables diseñadas por Jasper Morrison y fabricadas por Magis en polipropileno y fibra de vidrio.

FLARE
Designed by Marcel Wanders
Made by MAGIS
www.magisdesign.com

Fun table made with standard injection-moulded polycarbonate transparent clear. Tops in MDF with polymeric cover. Pattern options available: set of white sheets in art paper for customers own pattern, set of patterns by Marcel Wanders or set of patterns by Javier Mariscal.

Divertida mesa para habitación infantil o juvenil fabricada en policarbonato transparente modelado por inyección. Las patas están decoradas con estampados diseñados por diseñadores de prestigio internacional como Marcel Wanders o Javier Mariscal.

MAGIS WAGON
Designed by Michael Young
Made by MAGIS
www.magisdesign.com

Small table on wheels.
Material: frame in sand-blasted die-cast aluminium.
Container in standard injection-moulded ABS. Wheels in polyurethane.

Mesita con ruedas diseñada por Michael Young para Magis, moldeada por inyección y con ruedas de poliuretano.

AIR-TV TABLE
Designed by Jasper Morrison
Made by MAGIS
www.magisdesign.com

Small table on wheels. Complete with holder for videorecorder, dvd.
Material: polypropylene with glass fibre added. Air moulded. Holder for videorecorde in chromed steel rod.

Mesa pequeña con ruedas que se completa con una estantería metálica ideal para poner un reproductor de vídeo, dvd o la playstation.
Material: polipropileno con fibra de vidrio. Moldeado por aire. La estantería para sujetar el dvd está hecha de acero cromado.

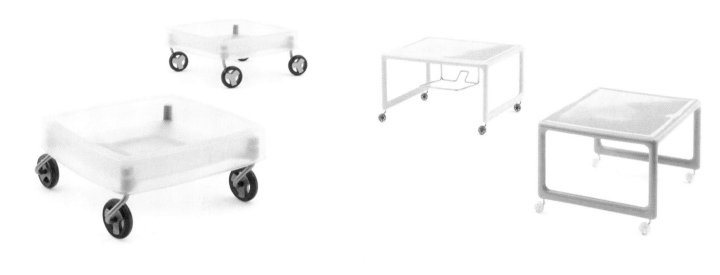

FLOWER TABLE
Designed by Christine Schwarzer
Made by SWEDESE
www.swedese.se

Originally created as a coffee table by designer Christine Schwarzer, it can also be used as a bedside table in a child's bedroom or as an amusing desk.

Concebida por la diseñadora Christine Schwarzer como mesa de café, también puede utilizarse como mesita de noche para la habitación infantil o como divertido escritorio.

CONVERTIBLE HIGH-CHAIR
Designed by Mi cuna
Made by MI CUNA
www.micuna.com

From Micuna, this practical highchair with its 3 position tray converts into a table and chair. Made from beech wood with screen printing, from the collection, on the table, the highchair – table is available in a wide range of colours, from strawberry, kiwi, mandarin, white, honey, natural, etc....

Mi cuna nos presenta esta funcional trona que se convierte en mesa silla, con una bandeja de 3 posiciones. Fabricada en madera de haya con la serigrafía de la colección en la mesa, la trona-mesa está disponible en una amplia gama de colores; desde fresa, kiwi, mandarina, blanco, miel, natural, etc...

ILUSIÓN
Designed by Mi Cuna
Made by MI CUNA
www.micuna.com

Designed originally as a cot, Ilusion can be later transformed into an amusing shelf unit when the baby grows. The cot base has two different height positions and the cot itself comes with an optional drawer.

Diseñado como una cuna, Ilusion se transforma en un divertido mueble estantería cuando el bebé crece. El somier tiene dos posiciones y se puede añadir un cajón opcional.

BIG NEMO
Designed by Mi cuna
Made by MI CUNA
www.micuna.com

From Micuna this wonderful cot is made from lacquered beech wood and converts into a small bed with two different base positions.

La firma Mi Cuna nos presenta esta estupenda cuna convertible en camita con dos posiciones de somier y fabricada en madera de haya y combinado en lacado.

COMBIDÚ
Designed by Mi cuna
Made by MI CUNA
www.micuna.com

The COMBIDÚ collection comes in a wide range of colours and is made with beech wood from sustainable forests.

La colección COMBIDÚ está diseñada en una amplia gama de colores utilizando maderas de haya provenientes de bosques sostenibles.

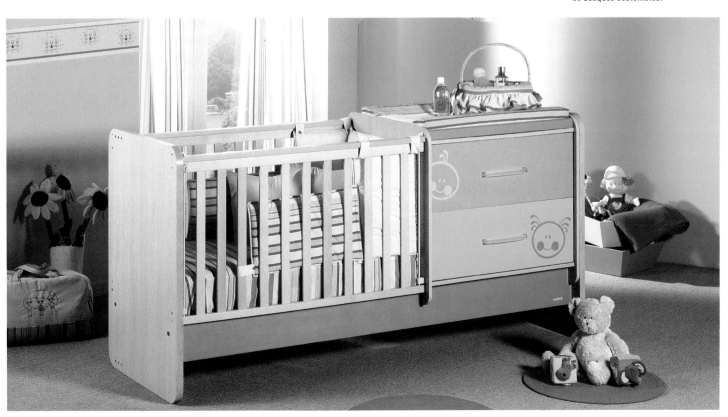

SCREWED
Designed by Ross Didier
Made by ROSS DIDIER
www.rossdidier.com

Designer Ross Didier bring us an interesting visual art piece and practical hook for hanging coats, umbrellas, bags and towels.
Materials: intended for injected moulded polymer and precision cast aluminium.

El diseñador Ross Didier nos presenta este interesante y divertido colgador en forma de tornillo, muy práctico para colgar la ropa, paragüas, o la cartera del colegio.
Materiales: polimero moldeado por inyección y aluminio.

VIRA SPOOL LAMP
Designed by Ronan & Erwan Bouroullec
Made by MALIN LUNDMARK
www.malinlundmark.com

A lamp made of glass, in the shape of a spool. The cord is kept around the shape, and you can roll out the length of the cord as long as you want. The cord also functions as decoration on the shape.

Original lámpara hecha de cristal con la forma de un carrete de hilo de coser. El cable se guarda enrollado alrededor del cuerpo de la lámpara y se puede estirar a la medida que necesitemos.

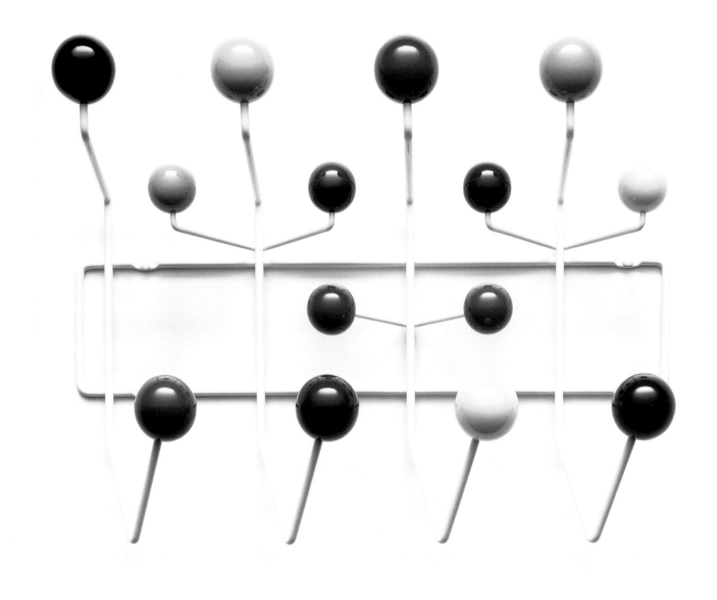

HANG IT ALL
Designed by Charles & Ray Eames
Made by VITRA
www.vitra.com

Used instead of simple hooks, these brightly-coloured wooden spheres were aimed at encouraging children to hang up "all their things". Because the distance between the spheres always remains the same, Hang it can be extended as required and is a cheerful alternative to boring clothes-hooks, not only for children's rooms. Collection Vitra Design Museum.

En lugar de sencillos ganchos, las bolas de madera de colores vivos pretenden animar a los niños, literalmente, a colgar "todas sus cosas" en este perchero. Dado que la distancia entre las bolas es siempre idéntica, Hang it all se puede ampliar a su gusto y constituye una alternativa divertida a los aburridos percheros, no sólo para la habitación infantil. Colección Vitra Design Museum.

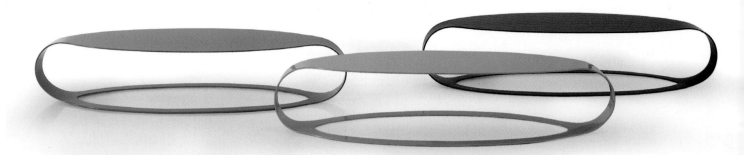

ORA L TABLE
Designed by Roberta Savelli
Made by SPHAUS
www.sphaus.com

Elliptical table in laser-cut peraluman aluminium plate, 6mm thick, modelled by hand. Automotive paint finish, hand-polished, with clear scratchproof coating.

Mesa con forma elípica realizada en aluminio de 6 milímetros de espesor, cortada con láser y modelada a mano. La pintura también ha sido pulida a mano.

MY 082
Designed by Michael Young
Made by MAGIS
www.magisdesign.com

A set of tables designed by Michael Young for prestigious company Magis. The rounded shapes and combination of brightly coloured legs makes them ideal for either children's or teenager's bedrooms.

Colección de mesas diseñadas por Michael Young para la prestigiosa firma Magis. Ideales para las habitaciones infatiles y juveniles gracias a sus formas redondeadas y a la combinación de las patas en colores llamativos.

ORA M TABLE
Designed by Roberta Savelli
Made by SPHAUS
www.sphaus.com

Elliptical table in laser-cut peraluman aluminium plate, 6mm thick, modelled by hand. Automotive paint finish, hand-polished, with clear scratchproof coating.

Mesita con forma elípica realizada en aluminio de 6 milímetros de espesor, cortada con láser y modelada a mano. Pintura pulida a mano.

SUSSEX
Designed by Robin Day
Made by MAGIS
www.magisdesign.com

Materials: frame in galvanized steel plate. Seat in polypropylene with glass fibre added. Air moulded. Suitable for floor-fixing. For outdoor use. Also available: linking device in zinc-plated steel plate.

Banco perfecto para la habitación de los más pequeños de la casa. Disponible en multitud de colores y además puede fijarse en el suelo.
Materiales: fabricado en acero galvanizado y polipropileno con fibra de vidrio.

HORNSLETH
Designed by Kristina von Hornsleth
Made by DNMARK
www.dnmark.com

Art meets design . Dnmark asked the internationally known artist and provocateur Kristian von Hornsleth to create a piece of furniture.
Whith inspiration from his paintings and architecture, Hornsleth has created a table that affers the user a different seating experience, without compromising functionality.

El arte se encuentra con el diseño. La firma Dnmark pidió al internacionalmente reconocido y provocador artista Kristian von Hornsleth que crease para ellos una pieza de mobiliario.
Inspirándose en sus pinturas y arquitectura, Hornsleth ha creado una mesa que incita a la persona que se sienta a jugar y experimentar, sin importarle demasiado la funcionalidad.

BOX
Designed by Ronan & Erwan Bouroullec
Made by VITRA
www.vitra.com

Box is a multifunctional storage unit that doubles up as a sidetable. Its soft rounded carcass is clad on the inside and outside with a fine woven fabric; cables can be slotted upwards through the cut-out in the top panel. In this way, a portable computer, a small TV, a reading lamp or a table fan can be placed on Box.

Box es al mismo tiempo un mueble multifuncional de almacenamiento y una mesa auxiliar. Un fino tejido de punto recubre la estructura, suavemente curvada, por dentro y por fuera; los cables se pueden llevar hacia arriba a través del hueco de la cubierta. De este modo, en Box se pueden instalar fácilmente un ordenador portátil, un pequeño aparato de televisión y una lámpara de lectura o un ventilador de sobremesa, por ejemplo.

FLOWER POT
Designed by Verner Panton
Made by BRANEX DESIGN
www.branexdesign.com

Designed by Verner Panton, the famous lamp owes its name at the unrestrained and merry "Flower Power" period. If the FlowerPot lamp shines, it is however not by its eccentricity. Proof that sobriety rhyme with originality! Vain and discrete in its table lamp or suspension version, it becomes impertinent and exuberant declined in candlestick. Material: FlowerPot Aluminium and Stainless Steel.

Diseñada por Verner Panton, la famosa lámpara debe su nombre al movimiento hippie de los años 70 "Flower Power". ¡La sobriedad rima con la originalidad!. También se encuentra su alter-ego en forma de lámpara de pie. Materiales: Aluminio y acero inoxidable.

SITUATION
Designed by Ronan & Erwan Bouroullec
Made by BOUROULLEC
www.bouroullec.com

The desk is made of Corian® and leather. The Corian® is smooth, deep, rather cold. The desk blotter is made of leather, a fine sheet laid into the desktop's surface. With this surface, the touch oscillates between hard and supple, between the plain synthetic material and the leather.

Bouroullec nos presenta este precioso escritorio realizado con Corian® y piel. El Corian® es de tacto suave y frío. La tabla del escritorio está semicubierta por un mantel de cuero que cae suavemente sobre la superficie de la mesa, creando un atractivo efecto junto con el material sintético de las patas y el tablero.

THE CUP LAMP
Designed by Malin Lundmark
Made by BOUROULLEC
www.malinlundmark.com

A lamp made of an old coffee cup. Hangs on the wall in its own ear. All the lamps are unique.

Preciosa lámpara hecha a partir de una taza de café antigua. Se puede colgar en la pared por su asa. Todas las lámparas de la colección son únicas.

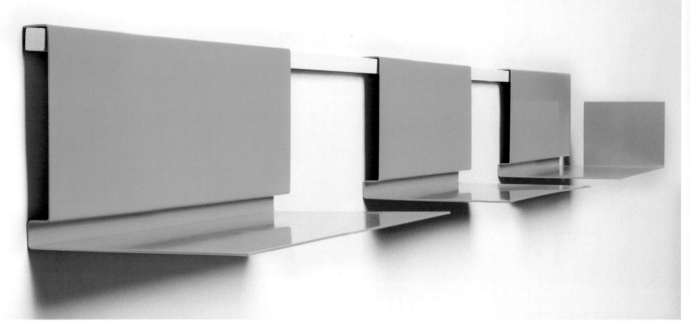

SHELVES
Designed by Konkret Form
Made by KONKRET FORM
www.konkretform.se

The shelves are a new product, mainly designed for cd´s and paperbacks, you can ad as many or few "shelfparts" as you wish on a simple metal grid.

Shelves fué diseñada principalmente para almacenar cd's, revistas o cómics. Se pueden añadir tantas piezas como se deseen en una simple rejilla metálica.

JIGSAW
Designed by Linde Hermans
Made by VLAEMSCH
www.vlaemsch.be

One flat piece of metal, in a L-form, with the ends of both legs welded in such a way that they join together again to form a cube and a table. An infinite number of the puzzles can be linked, to any sort of constellation.

Realizada en metal de una pieza en forma de L, está diseñanada para que al juntarse formen una mesa cuadrada. Una mesa que invita a jugar es perfecta para la habitación de los más pequeños.

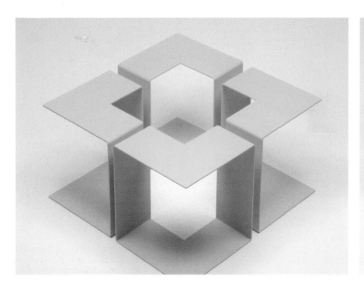

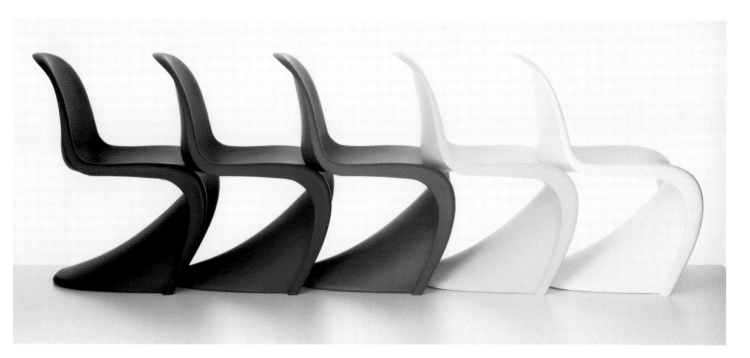

PANTON CHAIR CLASSIC
Designed by Verner Panton
Made by SPHAUS
www.sphaus.com

Danish designer Verner Panton spent many years thinking about how to produce a plastic chair moulded in one piece. Together with Vitra, he came up with the first prototypes in the 1960s and Panton Chair went into series production as of 1967. Unlike the cheaper Panton Chair Standard in solid plastic, PANTON CHAIR CLASSIC is made of rigid expanded plastic and has a lacquered surface.

El diseñador danés Verner Panton se dedicó durante muchos años al proyecto de fabricar una silla de plástico de una sola pieza. En colaboración con Vitra, en los años 60 se crearon los primeros prototipos; a partir de 1967, la Panton Chair se fabricó en serie. A diferencia de la Panton Chair Standard, íntegramente de plástico y más económica, la PANTON CHAIR CLASSIC está realizada en espuma dura y tiene una superficie barnizada.

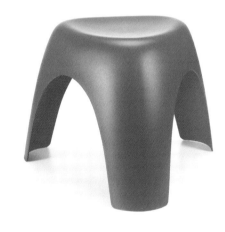

ELEPHANT STOOL
Designed by Sori Yanagi
Made by VITRA
www.vitra.com

The Elephant Stool is one of the most famous post-war Japanese designs and is still as convincing as ever with its clear formal idiom and great functionality. Suitable for indoors, balconies and gardens, the stacking stool can even be used as an easy-to-transport picnic stool.
Collection Vitra Design Museum.
Materials: polypropylene, dyed through.

El taburete Elefante es uno de los más famosos diseños japoneses, gracias a su forma y gran funcionalidad. Perfecto para interiores, pero también para balcones o jardines.
Colección Vitra Design Museum.
Materiales: polipropileno teñido.

EERO
Designed by Filippo Dell`Orto
Made by SPHAUS
www.sphaus.com

Rocking armachair in polyurethane foam reinforced by a steel tube frame.
Upholsetered with fabric or leather from catalogue. Polyurethane base.

Sillón mecedora fabricado en en espuma de poliuretano reforzada por un marco de acero. La base también es de poliuretano.

MINNI
Designed by Luisa Peixoto
Made by LUISA PEIXOTO
www.luisapeixotodesign.com

From Luisa Peixoto the Minni set comprises a minimalist style cot and dresser in pure white. The impression created by this pure simple design makes the baby's room appear to be that of an angel's bedroom up in the clouds.

Luisa Peixoto nos presenta la colección Minni compuesta por una cuna y un tocador de carácter minimalista en un blanco inmaculado. La pureza de las líneas y la limpieza del diseño hacen que la habitación del bebé parezca la habitación de un ángel en las nubes.

LIGHTCUBE
Designed by Konkret Form
Made by KONKRET FORM
www.konkretform.se

The lightcubes are designed to be as simple as it gets, the main design philosophy of all Konkret Form products.You can put them on the floor on a shelf/table or hang them from the roof, easy to use.
Material: White transparent acrylic.
H= 150mm,W= 150mm, D= 150mm.

Diseño sencillo es la filosofía de la firma Konkret Form para todos sus productos. Podemos colocar estos cubos de luz en el suelo o en una mesita o colgarlos en el techo ya que son muy fáciles de usar.
Material: Acrílico transparente.
H= 150mm W= 150mm D= 150mm.

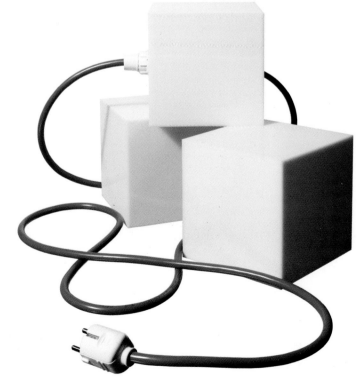

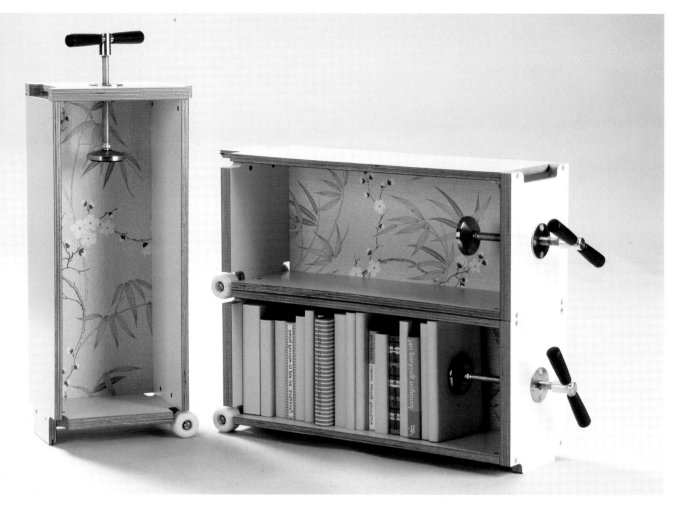

BOOKS-TO-GO!
Designed by Rose Cobb
Made by ROSE COBB
www.mo-billy.com

Aside from being a decorative element in its own right, this design from Rose Cobb will help us to keep our books in place and prevent them falling by securing them in a very special way. The easy way to make a game of teaching our children to keep their things tidy. Made from laminated plywood, steel and acrylic, this is without doubt state-of-the-art furniture for modern lifestyles.

Además de ser un elemento decorativo en si mismo, este diseño de Rose Cobb nos ayudará mantener los libros en su sítio sin que se caigan sujetándolos de una manera un tanto especial. La manera más fácil de educar jugando a nuestros hijos para que sean ordenados con sus cosas. Fabricado en contrachapado laminado, acero y acrílico. Sin duda es mobiliario de vanguardia para la vida moderna.

LIGHT CUBE MOOD
Designed by Viteo
Made by VITEO
www.viteo.at

A Plexiglas housing mounted on a stainless steel base envelops the hi-tech interior of the Viteo Light Cube "Mood". The Viteo Light Cube Mood enables you to create your own large number of lighting combinations by remote control (LED). Colours can be mixed and dimmed in various levels of intensity.

Alojado en el interior de un cubo de plexiglás y montado en una base de acero inoxidable se esconde la alta tecnología del Light Cube de Viteo. Nos permite crear un gran número de combinaciones y efectos lumínicos gracias a su mando a distancia. Los colores pueden ser mezclados y atenuados en varios niveles de intensidad.

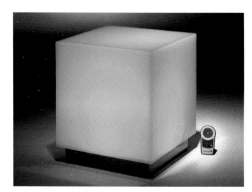

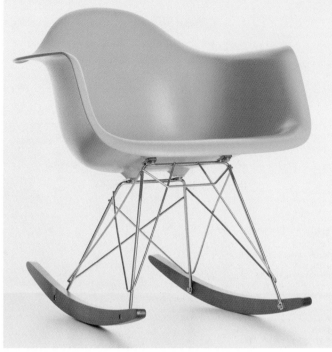

HOME DESK
Designed by George Nelson
Made by VITRA
www.vitra.com

Beautiful desktop designed by Gerge Nelson for Vitra.
Materials: chromed metal tubing. Writing surface in white laminate, wraparound wooden frame in veneered walnut.

Preciosa mesa de escritorio diseñada por George Nelson para Vitra.
Materiales: tubo metálico cromado. Superficie de escritura en laminado blanco, el marco decorativo es de madera chapada de nogal.

RAR
Designed by Charles & Ray Eame
Made by VITRA
www.vitra.com

Plastic Armchairs were first presented as part of the famed New York Museum of Modern Art competition, "Low Cost Furniture Design".
Materials: seat shell in polypropylene, dyed through, four-legged braced wire base on two wooden rockers with clear varnish.
RAR = Rocking Armchair Rod Base

Los sillones de plástico de Vitra fueron presentados como parte del concurso de Arte Moderno del Museo de Nueva York, "Diseño de Mobiliario de bajo coste".
Materiales: asiento de polipropleno teñido, patas de alambre y madera en barniz claro para los mecedores.

OENI
Designed by Philippe Allaeys
Made by Viteo
www.viteo.at

Children's wooden table with a blackboard top. A most entertaining way for the smallest members of the household to enjoy themselves in didactic play.

Mesa infantil de madera con tablero de pizarra. Una manera muy divertida de que los más pequeños de la casa se diviertan jugando de una manera didáctica.

CONTAINER TABLE
Designed by Marcel Wanders
Made by MOOOI
www.moooi.com

Simple forms for this table designed by Marcel Wanders for Moooi.
Material foot: PE, the foot can be filled with water to create extra stability.
Material top: a flat panel based on thermosetting resins, homogeneously reinforced with woodfibres and manufactured under high pressure and at high temperatures for outdoor use.

Mesitas de diseño simple diseñadas por Marcel Wanders para la firma Moooi.
Material pie: el pie se puede llenar de agua para proporcionar más estabilidad.
Material mesa: panel liso a base de resinas termofraguantes, reforzada con fibras de madera.

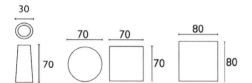

CORK FAMILY
Designed by Jasper Morrison
Made by VITRA
www.vitra.com

Three small friends, robustly built, stable, individual in character and lovable in appearance, that's the Cork Family. Whether as side-tables or as stools, the three different brothers benefit from the advantageous properties of the natural material: cork. It is comparatively light, enormously tough and has a pleasant soft feel.
Material: turned natural cork.

Tres pequeños amigos, robustos, estables, pero individuales en cuanto a carácter, esa es la familia Cork. Se pueden utilizar tanto como mesitas de noche como taburetes, los tres "hermanos" aunque distintos tienen algo en común: todos están fabricados con corcho. Son ligeros, enormemente resistentes y dan una sensación suave y agradable.
Material: corcho natural.

BIG NUVE
Designed by Mi cuna
Made by MI CUNA
www.micuna.com

This cot converts into a bed with a choice of two base heights and an optional drawer. The bed measures 140x70cm, the cot 140x70cm and the drawer 131x52 cm.

Cuna convertible en cama con dos posiciones de somier y un cajón opcional. Las medidas de la cama son de 140x70cm, la cuna serían 140x70cm y el cajón 131x52 cm.

DREAM
Designed by Mi cuna
Made by MI CUNA
www.micuna.com

DREAM is a collection which comes from Micuna, specialists in children's furniture. Made from beech wood, the collection is available in a choice of two colours, kiwi and ocean.

DREAM es la colección que nos presenta la firma Mi Cuna, especialistas en mobiliario infantil. Se presenta en colores kiwi y océano y están fabricada con madera de haya.

free time for everybody

tiempo libre para todos

Doubtless nobody ever questions the right for children to have their own leisure zone. But what about the adults? It could be said that we not only have the right to our own rest and relaxation zone but that we positively need it.

The hectic pace of modern lifestyles takes it toll equally on our minds as our bodies and more and more we look to the comfort of our own homes as a refuge, a place to relax and escape the pressures of adult life.

Through a meticulous selection of the latest in comfortable furniture designs from the best international designers this chapter explores the idea of those areas in the home where we choose to relax amongst family or friends, literally the place we spend the majority of our time at home.

Sin duda, nadie cuestiona el derecho a disponer de un espacio propio para ocio de los niños. Pero ¿y los adultos?. Posiblemente no solo tengamos derecho a nuestro espacio de ocio, sino que lo necesitamos.

El ajetreado ritmo de vida actual, repercute tanto en nuestro cuerpo como en nuestra mente, y cada vez más nos refugiamos en el confort de nuestra casa para relajarnos y escapar de la tensión de la vida adulta.

Este capítulo explora la idea del espacio dentro del hogar donde nos relajamos en familia o con amigos, lugares donde pasamos la mayor parte del tiempo en nuestras casas, a través de una selección minuciosa de mobiliario confortable y de última generación en diseño, de los mejores creadores internacionales.

CONCO!
Designed by Michiel van der Kley
Made by ARTIFORT
www.artifort.com
www.michielvanderkley.com

Could a chair be as streamlined as the body of an aeroplane?
A body that looks rounded, similar to a boulder being eroded
for a long time in the sea before it reaches its ultimate shape.
The base strengthens the lightness of the design by its shape.
The knot is an aesthetical feature but also a technical detail.
On the one side a point where all the curved lines meet and on
the other side a place where the fabric can be held together.

¿Puede una silla ser tan aerodinámica como el cuerpo de un
avión? Un cuerpo de aspecto redondeado, similar a un canto
rodado erosionado durante mucho tiempo por el mar. La base
de esta silla refuerza la ligereza de su diseño. El nudo es un
detalle estético y técnico a la vez. Por un lado un punto en el
que convergen todas las líneas curvas y por otro es el punto de
fijación de la tela.

CLEO
Designed by MODOLOCO
Made by SPHAUS
www.sphaus.com

Cleo is a light for the desk or bedside table: a painted steel
rods structure support a simple diffuser screen made of white
polycarbonate.

Cleo es una lámpara para el escritorio o para la mesita de
noche: una base de metal pintado sirve como soporte a una
simple pantalla difusora hecha con policarbonato blanco.

COLLECTION BERTOIA
Designed by Harry Bertoia
Made by KNOLL STUDIO
www.knoll.com

Harry Bertoia's 1952 experiment bending metal rods into practical art produced a revered collection of seating, including this previously unreleased piece. Fifty years on and the designs created by Bertoia still continue to be one of the most avant-garde and industrially manufactured concepts. The Bertoia collection is perfect for our sitting room.

A mediado de los años cincuenta el diseñador Harry Bertoia realizó un experimento doblando varas de metal produciendo una aclamada colección de sillas. Cincuenta años después el diseño creado por Bertoia sigue siendo uno de los coceptos más vanguardistas e industrialmente producido. La colección Bertoia es ideal para nuestra sala de estar.

T-AROUND THE ROSES
Designed by Luca Nichetto & Massimo Gardone
Made by MOROSO
www.moroso.it

Low tables with a high technological content thanks to the use of Alicrite for both the version with two-tone layers and the one with an incorporated, dyesublimation-printed fabric with a flower-inspired pattern created by Massimo Gardone. This acrylic material is resistant to chemicals, such as acids, alkalis, oils, petrol. This exclusive technology was developed in co-operation with Lisa Tavazzani, expert product manager.

Mesas bajas con un alto contenido tecnológico gracias al uso del Alicrite, tanto para la versión en dos capas de distinto tono, como para la que va forrada con tela y la versión impresa con motivos florales diseñanda por Massimo Gardonde. Este material acrílico es muy resistente a productos químicos, como ácidos, petróleo o gasolina. Esta exclusiva tecnología fue desarrollada con la cooperación de Lisa Tavazzani, experta en diseño de producto.

ONE TWO THREE
Designed by Domodinamica
Made by DOMODINAMICA
www.domodinamica.com

One Two Three is a versatile lamp reflecting the play of light. Less is more.

One Tow Three es una lámpara muy versatil reflejando y jugando con la luz. Menos es más.

EASY SLEEP
Designed by Luca Scacchetti
Made by DOMODINAMICA
www.domodinamica.com

Sofa realized in polyurethane resins shaped and bending on itself. When occurred can be opened and transformed in bed. Covering by joining of fabric and leather like per sample collection. This sofa is ideal for rest and relaxation zones since it can, if need be, be converted into a bed, perfect for when we have guests.
W=200, D=115/215, H=77 cm

Sofa fabricado con resinas de poliuretano. Ideal para las zonas de ocio ya que si se quiere este sofá puede convertirse en cama, ideal para cuando tenemos invitados.
W=200, D=115/215, H=77 cm

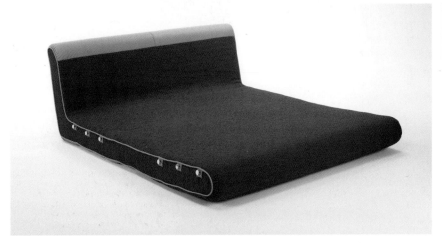

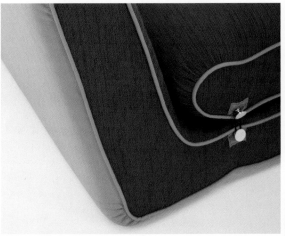

PLUS UNIT
Designed by Werner Aisslinger
Made by MAGIS
www.magisdesign.com

System of drawer units in ABS. Stacking and adjoining. Available on feet or wheels.
Material: drawer units in standard injection-moulded polished ABS. Runners in polished extruded aluminium.
Caps in polished aluminium or painted aluminium in the same colour as the drawer.

Sistema de unidades de cajón en ABS apilados entre si. Está diseñado con ruedas y también hay una versión con pies.
Materiales: los cajones estan moldeados por inyección y pulido ABS. Las guías han sido diseñadas en aluminio.

VOIDO
Designed by Ron Arad
Made by MAGIS
www.magisdesign.com

Rocking chair. Comfortable for watching TV, reading or just relaxing, this rocking chair is perfect for the room in the house destined to rest and relaxation, although it can also be used outdoors.

Silla balancín. Muy comoda para ver la televisión, leer, o simplemente descansar, es una silla perfecta para la habitación de la casa destinada al ocio y al relax, aunque también se puede utilizar en exteriores.
Materiales: polietileno moldeado.

MOLLIO
Designed by Anne Georg
Made by ANNE GEORG
www.annegeorg.com

Mollio is a sofa/an easy chair designed for public as well as domestic use. It is fashioned to fulfil human comfort within three different subjects; physical and mental comfort along with flexibility. Mollio is a concept built upon three easy chairs which can be combined into a sofa, a lounge suite or individual seating.

Mollio es un conjunto de tres sillas que se combinan entre si formando un sofá, una chaise lounge para el salón o asientos individuales. Mollio es un concepto diseñado para un total comfort en todos los sentidos: físico y mental.

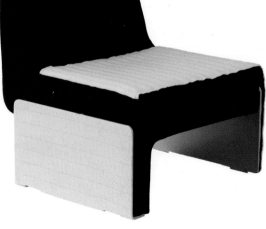

KAAR
Designed by Setsu e Shinobu Ito
Made by SPHAUS
www.sphaus.com

KAAR is a contemporary version of the classic étagère. Composed by curved plywood modules finished with matt anti scratch lacquer. They're assebled together trough a free   rotatory joint: this allows the maximum flexibility of use and aesthetic.

KAAR es una versión contemporanea del clásico étagère. Formado por módulos de contrachapado curvados con un acabado mate antirasguños. Están unidos gracias a una rótula giratoria libre, lo que permite una flexibilidad absoluta de su uso y de la estética.

INTERFACE
Designed by Matali Crasset
Made by DOMODINAMICA
www.domodinamica.com

The structure of this armchair is stuffed by polyurethane expanded. It is supported by steel chromed brushed feet.The various angles - form permit the construction of compositions able to offer interfacing and interlocutories position. The small pouff, realized by the same material, completes the system permitting the wished opproaching. Patented.
The colour marching permits to follow the composition of chair system by continuous changing.
W=58, D=75, H=115 cm
W=30, D=20, H=35 cm

La estructura de este sillón ha sido rellenada de poliuretano expandido. Se apoya en unas patas fabricadas de acero cromado. Los diversos ángulos y colores en los que ha sido diseñado permiten diferentes composiciones. El pequeño puf también se ha realizado en el mismo material que las sillas.
W=58 D=75 H=115 cm
W=30 D=20 H=35 cm

RIPPLE CHAIR
Designed by Ron Arad
Made by MOROSO
www.moroso.it

The frame of Ripple Chair is made of white polished and natural injection-moulded thermoplastic to highlight the design in relief that is reminiscent of the traces left by sea waves on sand. The circular aperture of the seat, the lightness and softness of the lines, the sturdiness of the material used and its stackability make Ripple Chair particularly suitable for both domestic and public spaces.
Characteristics:
Shell of polypropylen.
Basement in varnished white or black mat, chromed or stainless 316 L steel.
Underfoot in polyethylene.

El marco de la Ripple Chair está moldeado por inyección termoplástica para destacar el diseño con reminiscencias que nos recuerdan al rastro dejado por las olas del mar en la arena. La abertura circular del asiento, la ligereza, la suavidad de las líneas, la fuerza de los materiales empleados y su facilidad de apilarse hacen de la Ripple Chair un objeto perfecto tanto para interiores domésticos como para espacios públicos.
Características:
Silla en polipropileno.
Base de acero inoxidable barnizado en blaco o negro.
Tapas de las patas de polietileno.

KIRK!
Designed by René Holten
Made by ARTIFORT
www.artifort.com

Hanging in space, free-floating on a slender landing-gear. Designed by René Holten. A strong arm-chair with a clear character. Love it or hate it. Ideal for Lobbies, lounges or talk-shows, Kirk is certainly an eye-catcher. A deep, comfortable seat with a surprisingly good back support.
Material: metal frame with tubular base. Swivelling with a self-return mechanism.

Diseñado por René Holten, este sillón parece que flote libremente en el espacio. Un confortable sillón con mucha personalidad, lo puedes amar o lo puedes odiar. Es perfecto para vestíbulos, salones, e ideal para las habitaciones destinadas al ocio en casa. Está claro que Kirk no pasará desapercibido.
Material: marco de metal con base tubular. Giración con mecanismo autovuelta.

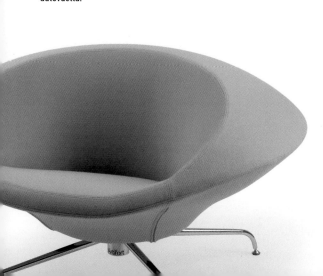

BERTOIA ASYMMETRIC CHAISE
Designed by Harry Bertoia
Made by KNOLL STUDIO
www.knoll.com

Harry Bertoia designed the ASYMMETRIC CHAISE in the early 1950s, but the chair was never produced beyond the prototypical form. Sculptural, airy, and breathtaking in shape and form, the Asymmetric Chaise is considered to be a masterpiece of mid-century american furniture. Available in chrome or white outdoor finish. The ASYMMETRIC CHAISE can be specified unupholstered, with a seat cushion, or with a full cover.

Harry Bertoia diseño la ASYMMETRIC CHAISE a principio de los años cincuenta, pero la silla nunca fué reproducida en su forma prototípica. Escultural, ventilada e impresionante en su forma, la ASYMMETRIC CHAISE se considera como la obra maestra del mobiliario americano de mediados del siglo veinte. Está disponible en cromo o en color blanco.

PLATNER DINING AND LOW TABLES
Designed by Warren Platner
Made by KNOLL STUDIO
www.knoll.com

Ideal for any office lounge or residence . Available as dining table, side table and coffee table. Available on the KnollStudio 20 day program in select sizes and finishes. Base features a clear plastic extrusion ring that creates a smooth bottom surface Top features 3/8"-thick tempered glass. Clear glass top finish. Vertical steel wire rods have bright nickel finish with clear lacquer protection.

Ideal como mesa de reuniones, también está disponlible una versión como mesa de comedor, mesita de café y mesa auxiliar. En el anillo metalico base se ha dispuesto una goma gruesa para que la mesa se apoye suavemente en el suelo. Las varas de alambre de acero verticales, que forman el cuerpo de la mesa, se protegen gracias a un barniz de alta protección.

FLOOD LIGHT
Designed by Mathias Cross
Made by WOK
www.wokmedia.com

A light that explores our nervousness around electricity, addressing it with a childish naivety using the archetype of a light bulb in water and apparently shoddy wiring to produce an icon of a 'bad idea' that works despite itself. FLOOD LIGHT is a serious proposition for a product, it is fascinating and beautiful and can be placed in the home. Only the idea is dangerous, not the product.

FLOOD LIGHT has sido diseñada por Mathias Cross para la firma Wok, inspirado en el miedo que tenemos desde la infancia acerca del peligro de sumergir cualquier objeto conectado a la electricidad en agua. El FLOOD LIGHT se puede instalar perfectamente en casa, sólo la idea es peligrosa, el producto es totalmente seguro e increíblemente decorativo.

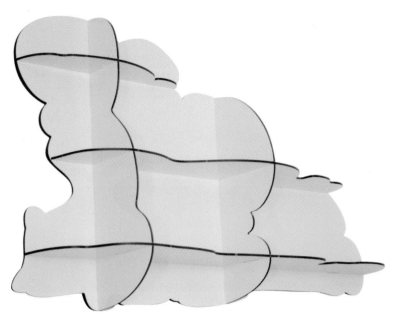

NIMBUS
Designed by Ibride
Made by IBRIDE
www.ibride.fr

This very decorative shelving unit, brought to us from French company Ibride, simulates a cloud in the heavens and has the storage capacity for fifty DVD's or paperbacks. The perfect solution for keeping the house's leisure room in order.

La estantería que nos presenta la firma francesa Ibride simula una nube situada en las alturas, es muy decorativa y tiene capacidad de almacenar mas de medio centenar de dvd o libros de bolsillo. Ideal para mantener todo en orden en la habitación de la casa destinada al ocio.
W=108 D=22 H=64 cm

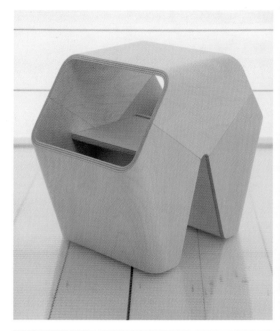

SHIPSHAPE
Designed by Isokon Plus
Collaboration with Tomoko Azumi
Made by AZUMI
www.shinazumi.com

This amusing piece of furniture makes an ideal and handy magazine rack although it also serves as a seat, occasional table or improvised bedside table. Since it takes up very little room it's also perfect for smaller spaces.

Este divertido mueble es ideal como práctico revistero, aunque hace las veces de asiento, mesa auxiliar o improvisada mesita de noche. Al no ocupar mucho espacio es perfecta para espacios reducidos.
W=450 D=295 H=400 mm

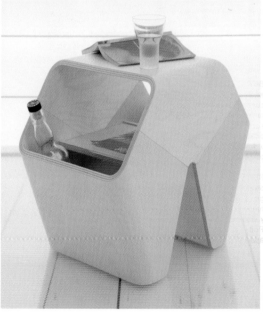

COFFE TABLE
Designed by Suck UK
Made by SUCK UK
www.suck.uk.com

Designed by English firm Suck UK, this brilliant little stainless steel and glass table is illuminated by a fluorescent light. It is also possible to personalize the drawing, design or photograph which is screen printed onto the table's glass.

La firma inglesa Suck UK ha diseñado esta genial mesita de acero inoxidable y cristal iluminada con luz florescente. Se puede personalizar el dibujo, diseño o fotografía que se serigrafiará en el cristal que hace de mesa.

MARSHMALLOW SOFA
Designed by George Nelson
Made by VITRA
www.vitra.com

Nelson's design transformed the traditional sofa into a three-dimensional pattern consisting of 18 brightly-coloured sections of upholstery, supported by a simple steel structure. This unusual shape and construction make Marshmallow Sofa one of design history's more unusual sofas. An extension element consisting of six individual cushions can be mounted between two sofas, allowing sofa to be extended as required.

El diseño de Nelson Transformó el sofá tradicional en un objeto tridimensional consistente en 18 secciones de tapicería llenas de color, apoyadas en una simple estructura de acero. Esta forma inusual hacen que el sofá "golosina" sea uno de los sofás más atrevidos de la historia del diseño de mobiliario. Gracias a un elemento de extensión, que consiste en seis cojines individuales, se pueden unir dos sofás, permitiendo ampliar el sofá tantas veces como se desee.

BOVIST
Designed by Hella Jongeriusz
Made by VITRA
www.vitra.com

BOVIST is a decorative floor cushion, stool, and ottoman all in one. Its appealing shape and high degree of seating comfort are thanks to the large number of taken-in strips on the side and a filling of small plastic balls. Large sections of embroidery give the cover, which consists of different coloured fabrics, a particular charm and there is a knitted thread handle for moving Bovist to different places in the apartment.

BOVIST es un decorativo cojín para el suelo, taburete, y otomano todo en uno. Su atractiva forma y su comidad gracias a su relleno de pequeñas pelotas de plástico. Se ha diseñado en patchwork, con telas de colores diferentes y vistosos bordados, dándole un encanto muy particular. Podemos mover fácilmente el Bovist por todo el apartamento gracias a un mango de hilo tejido.

SOFA COMPACT
Designed by Charles & Ray Eames
Made by VITRA
www.vitra.com

In the shape of Compact Sofa, Charles and Ray Eames put a design originally intended for their own house in California into series production. Unusually high and divided into two horizontal strips, the backrest lends the sofa an interesting profile and clearly sets it apart from the weightiness of traditional sofas. The sofa can be folded up, making it easy to transport.
Material: chromed tubular metal frame, continuous polyurethane foam upholstery in three sections.

Inicialmente diseñado por Charles y Ray Eames para su propia casa en California, el SOFA COMPACT se fabricó en serie a mediado de los años sesenta. Su atractivo reside en la inusual altura de su resplado y en el estampado de líneas horizontales multicolor, lo que le hace totalmente distinto de los pesados sofás tradicionales. El sofá se puede plegar fácilmente lo que facilita enormemente su transporte.
Material: marco de metal tubular cromado, tapicería de espuma de poliuretano en tres secciones.

SWING
Designed by Denis Santachiara
Made by DOMODINAMICA
www.domodinamica.com

Structure stuffed by expanded polyurethane and Dacron. Swinging base in grey metalized ABS. Cover by unlinable fabric. It's a footless armchair that rests on only one point. It rotates and swivels. It rocks you in every directions even sideways. To read play, or dream on.
W=83 D=83 H=87 cm
W=50 D=50 H=45 cm

La estructura del sillón Swing diseñado por Denis Santachiara está rellena de poliuretano y Dacron. La base se balancea y está fabircada en ABS gris metalizado. El swing no tiene patas y descansa en un solo punto giratorio. Está diseñado para que pueda balancearse en todas direcciones. Perfecto para leer, jugar o dormir.
W=83 D=83 H=87 cm
W=50 D=50 H=45 cm

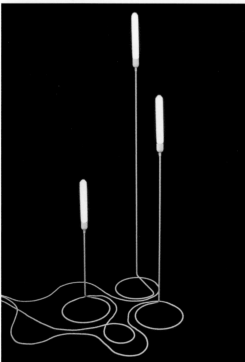

CORD LIGHT
Designed by Form Us With Love
Made by FORM US WITH LOVE
www.formuswithlove.se

From a snake nest of winding cords, this lamp shoots straight up and stands tall on it´s own. Surprising the eye by challenging the unexpected, the Cord Light is simple, yet characteristic. The cord, one of the most disturbing decorating details has been made useful. The lamp comes in small, medium or large, take your pick.

Form Us With Love nos presente este exquisita familia de lámparas. De diseño muy simple, el cable, uno de los detalles decorativos más incómodos y antiestéticos se ha convertido en algo útil y decorativo.

AMOEBE
Designed by Verner Panton
Made by VITRA
www.vitra.com

The Amoebe was originally dreamed up for Panton's famous Visiona installation. It is a marvellous example of close-to-the-floor lounge furniture and embodies the spirit of the early 1970s. In bright colours, the re-edition delivers even greater comfort thanks to its flexible backrest shell.
Materials: laminated structure, foam upholstery.

El espíritu de principio de los años setenta invade el diseño de este sillón, cuya particularidad es que no tiene patas y su propia estructura descansa en el suelo. Esta re-edición ha sido fabricada en colores vivos y con un respaldo muy flexible.
Materiales: estructura laminada, tapicería de espuma.

HM30
Designed by Hitch Mylius
Collaboration with Tomoko Azumi
Made by AZUMI
www.shinazumi.com

A range of sofa and table. When it is attached together, they look calm suite. However, when one sofa is installed individually, it evokes a sculptural quality - looks as if it is free from gravity and floating on one leg.
W=1200 D=750 H=700 mm

Conjunto de sofá y mesa de la firma Azumi diseñada por Hitch Mylius. Cuando la mesa y el sofá estan unidos la sensación que nos da es la de una sala de estar tranquila y ordenada, en cambio, si los despegamos el sofá parece que juega contra la fuerza de la gravedad y flote sobre una sola pata.
W=1200 D=750 H=700 mm

HIDDEN
Designed by Cross/Mathias
Made by WOK
www.wokmedia.com

The table was made as a series of project themes around childhood. The table (calls Hidden) uses the theme of hidding, not just for children to hide in, but to hide all the things adults do under tables, or to make secret stores of things tied into the jungle of string.

La mesa, inspirada en los juegos de nuestra infancia, nos transporta a un mundo de imaginación. Nos invita a escondernos, no solo a los niños, sino a los adultos, un pequeño y secreto escondrijo, una jungla hecha de cuerdas de colores ácidos.

BIG ARM
Designed by Bruehl
Collaboration with Tomoko Azumi
Made by AZUMI
www.shinazumi.com

An arm chair with a wide surfaced arm and the whole chair is on a swivel axis. Therefore, when it is rotated, one arm can be used as a work top for lap top computer, and user can lean against anther arm.
Material: upholstery with steel structure, washable cover.
W=900 D=800 H=700 mm

Azumi nos presenta este sillón de brazo amplio que gira sobre si mismo gracias a un eje giratorio. Es ideal para trabajar con un ordenador portátil ya que podemos utilizar uno de los brazos como mesita improvisada y el otro brazo como respaldo. Sin dua un sillón que hará las delicias en nuestros ratos de ocio.
Material: tapicería extraíble y lavable, estructura de acero.

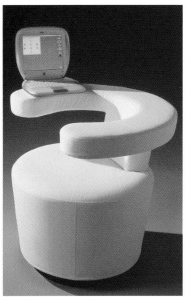

X3 STACKING CHAIR
Designed by Marco Maran
Made by KNOLL STUDIO
www.knoll.com

Stacks 15 on the floor. Comfortable with unique flex in the back. Ideal for cafe, residential and educational applications. X3 is a one-piece shell, obtained by the bi-injection of transparent polycarbonate and a desmopan colored lattice. The complex molding technology, applied for the first time to furniture, brings a unique, versatile effect to the chair. Chrome plated steel base.

Diseño confortable gracias al respaldo flexibe de esta silla ideal para sentarse en los ratos de ocio en casa, aunque también están diseñadas para su uso en cafeterías o en escuelas. La silla X3 está fabricada por bi-inyección de policarbonato transparente en una sola pieza. Esta compleja tecnología de moldeado, aplicada por primera vez en mobiliario, aporta un efecto único a la silla. Las patas son de acero plateado cromado.

K6-ML
Designed by Karim Rashid
Made by AITALI
www.karimrashid.com
www.aitali.com

Designed in acid colours by well known designer Karim Rashid, the K6-ML table is the perfect choice for lounges and the perfect way to add a touch of brightness and colour. The base and the X shaped legs are made from stainless steel.

Diseñada en colores ácidos por el reconocido diseñador Karim Rashid, la mesa K6-ML es perfecta para su uso en salas de estar, aportando un toque de color y luminosidad al espacio. Las base y las patas en forma de equis están fabricadas en acero inoxidable.

002.09
Designed by Filippo Dell´Orto
Made by SPHAUS
www.sphaus.com

Table with steel frame, chrome-plated or powder-coated in variety of colours. MDF table top reinforced by two aluminium plates. The chrome-plated frame version has a polyester-coated top laminated with a mirror-finish aluminium plate on the underside. The version with a coated frame has a matt polyurethane lacquered tabletop.
Dim. 280/240 X 100, h 73cm.

Mesa fabricada con marco de acero plateado o en una gran variedad de colores. El tablero de la mesa se ha realizado con MDF, reforzado con dos platos de aluminio. Los colores ácidos con los que ha sido diseñada aportan luz y profundidad en cualquier espacio en el que la coloquemos.

LA MICHETTA
Designed by Gaetano Pesce
Made by MERITALIA
www.meritalia.it

"La michetta" is the most simple and least expensive bread baked in Milan. No two michettas are ever the same, and even when baked in tins, they always take on different shapes during rising and baking. Meritalia offers "La michetta" as a system of modular components, though mass-produced with industrial processes, it always remains unique due to the different arrangements and different manufacturing methods used for the individual elements – just like michettas. LA MICHETTA is characterized by the variety of compositions that can be achieved by simply grouping the individual pieces chosen in a free, personal way, with no preset scheme and no limitations.

"La michetta" es el pan horneado más sencillo y barato en Milán. No hay dos Michettas iguales, aunque se horneen en moldes, siempre adoptan formas distintas durante la cocción. Meritalia nos presente su particular Michetta con un sistema de módulos, que aunque fabricados en serie con procesos industriales, cada módulo se individualiza de los otros gracias a los distintos arreglos que se le da a cada uno. LA MICHETTA se caracteriza por la variedad de composiciones que se pueden conseguir simplemente agrupando los diferentes módulos entre sí, obteniendo infinitas formas y espacios.

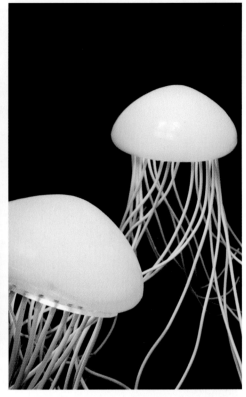

JELLYFRIENDS LIGHTS
Designed by Form us with love
Made by FORUM US WITH LOVE
www.forumuswithlove.se

JellyFriends is a quietly pulsating light armature that inte-
racts with the user and reacts when someone comes near.
The JellyFriends shaped body is moulded in silicone and
comes with adjustable silicone cord legs that enables a
unique expression of each JellyFriends. JellyFriends explore
the boundries between artefact and man and advocates a
living, dynamic environment.

JellyFriends es una lámpara con forma de medusa de mar y
está fabricada en su totalidad con silicona. Esta peculiar
lámpara interactúa con el usuario encendiéndose sola
cuando alquien se acerca.

AIR LOUNGE SYSTEM
Designed by Favio Novembre
Made by MERITALIA
www.meritalia.it

Italian designer Favio Novembre has designed this
table and integrated seat for Meritalia which also
serves as an armchair. The Air Lounge System is
the perfect armchair for reading, studying or playing video games.

El diseñador italiano Favio Novembre ha diseñado
para la frima Meritalia esta mesa con asiento
intergrado que puede hacer las veces de sillón. El
Air Lounge System es un sillón ideal para la
lectura, estudiar o para jugar a los videojuegos.

BOOGIE WOOGIE
Designed by Stefano Giovannoni
Made by MAGIS
www.magisdesign.com

Shelving system. Stacking and adjoining. Available with and without back panel. The modules cannot be fixed to the wall. All compositions must be placed on the ground. Material: standard injection-moulded glossy ABS.

Sistema de estanterias ajustables y apilables entre sí. Los modulos no se pueden fijar en la pared así que estos descansan directamente en el suelo.
Material: modelado ABS brillante por inyección.

WINNIE
Designed by Feld
Made by FELD
www.feld.com

Winnie is a comfortable swinging pouf which makes you rock. This fun shape allows you and your kids to rock at any time, at any place. Link them and you even have more fun. Available in wool and leather coverings.

Winnie es un confortable y cómodo pouf balanceable. Esta divertida forma permite que los niños se balanceen en cualquier momento y en cualquier lugar. Diseñados con fundas de cuero o lana.

POPUP
Designed by Feld
Made by FELD
www.feld.com

POPUP is a light and versatile seat, 2 positions, pouf or lounger. Fasten your seat belts, you have a lounger. Popup is ideal for relaxing in the kids room, TV-room, study room, or other cosy places. The seat is delivered as pouf in a box.

POPUP es un asiento ligero y versátil, dos posiciones, pouf o sillón. Es ideal para el cuarto de los niños, en el estuido o cualquier rincón de la casa destinado al relax o el ocio.

TROY
Designed by Bert der Aa
Made by ARTIFORT
www.artifort.it

TROY is a luxurous and comfortable chair for a modern but also classical surrounding. Characteristic through its trapezium-formed shell. The Troy family has different options for the base: 4-legged, sledge and rocking. Combined with a high or low back. The chair is applicable for residential as well as for contract market. Can be upholstered in several fabrics and leathers.

TROY es una silla de lujo muy cómoda que se ajusta a la perfección tanto en los entornos modernos como en los más clásicos. Se caracteriza por su forma de trapecio. La familia Troy dispone de diferentes opciones para su base: cuatro patas, trineo o mecedora. Puede tapizarse en varios tejidos y cuero.

CALLA
Designed by Stefano Giovannoni
Made by DOMODINAMICA
www.domodinamica.com

Armchair in polyuretane resins cold foamed in die is supported by a rotating base in polyshed aluminium alloy. It is covered eith elastic fabrics and offers the possibility to be transformed in chaise longue by suitables joints arrangin the arms overall opening as well as different positions in very good comfort. Take a seat into calla's soft petals.
Dimensions: 98(W) X 85(D) X 104,5(H) cm.

Sillón fabricado con resinas de poliuretano con una base rotante en aleación de aluminio. Forrado con tela elástica, ofrece la posibiliad de transformalo en una chaise longue gracias a la movilidad de sus brazos móviles. Su diseño se inspira en los pétalos suaves y dúctiles de las flores.
Dimensiones: 98(W) X 85(D) X 104,5(H) cm.

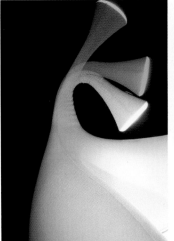
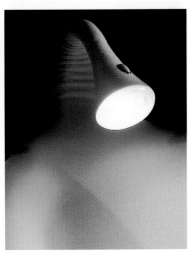

MORFEO

**Designed by Stefano Giovannoni
& Rodrigo Torres**
Made by DOMODINAMICA
www.domodinamica.com

Structure made of flexible polyurethane resin covered with
elastic fabrics as per sample collection. Inside the frame a
folding bed-net with mattress laid upon and it is easy to take
out. On head-sides two adjustables lamps provided with
switches offer a pleasant light. He is the God of sleep and he
has two long, luminous antennas, cuddle up into his arms
and you will have golden dreams.
W=200 D=90 H=80/145 cm
W=200 D=226 H=80/145 cm

La estructura está hecha de resina flexible de poliuretano
forrada con telas elásticas. Se trata de un sofá cama muy
sencillo de utilizar. A los lados encontramos dos lámparas
que ofrecen una luz muy agradable especialmente para la
lectura. Es el Dios del sueño y tiene dos largas y luminosas
antenas, acurrúcate en sus brazos y tendrás sueños de oro.
W=200 D=90 H=80/145 cm
W=200 D=226 H=80/145 cm

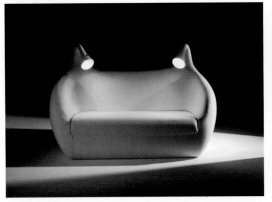

SHOWER OF LIGHT
Designed by Union
Made by AZUMI
www.shinazumi.com

The dimmer switch of this lighting system has been transformed into a shower tap. The shape of the tap suggests an obvious and delicate way of controlling the strength of a current. This small conversion not only invites functional advantage, but also opens our imagination: we feel that we are bathed in light like the water from a showerhead.
W=370 D=375 H=2000 mm

El interruptor de este sistema de iluminación ha sido transformado en un grifo de ducha. La forma de grifo sugiere una obvia y delicada manera de controlar la intensidad de la luz, y a la vez hacer volar nuestra imaginación sintiendo que nos duchamos con la luz.
W=370 D=375 H=2000 mm

working at home

trabajando en casa

The following pages aim to be of assistance to the growing population which has decided to create an area within their homes in which to carry out their working activities, work and home life happily sharing in the relaxed atmosphere and freedom offered by the family home.
The choice of furniture is designed to provide ideas and inspiration when it comes to the task of creating these areas and, with this aim in mind, the personal vision of the designers, their suggestions and latest design works provide an effective contribution.

Las siguientes páginas pretenden ser una ayuda para ese creciente grupo de personas, que han decidido crear en su casa un espacio reconfortante para el ejercicio de una actividad laboral y hacerla convivir felizmente con la relajada y más libre faceta de la vida hogareña.
La selección del mobiliario responde al objeto de sugerir e inspirar en la tarea de creación de estos espacios, donde la personal visión de los diseñadores con sus propuestas y últimos trbajos colaboran eficazmente a este fín.

SHORT DOUBLE DRAWER UNIT
Designed by Johannes Norlander
Made by ASPLUND
www.asplund.org

The Asplund Collection is a collection of modern high-quality products with roots in Swedish tradition and handicraft. The essence of the collection is functional, clean shaped, and elegant products with a Swedish-internatinoal feel.

La Colección Asplund es una colección de productos de alta calidad muy modernos con raíces de la artesanía tradicional Sueca. La esencia de la colección es la funcionalidad, de   líneas pura, y productos elegantes con un toque internacional.

LOW ARCHIVE DOOR UNIT
Designed by Johannes Norlander
Made by ASPLUND
www.asplund.org

CABINET LC/LD
Designed by Jonas Bohlin and
Thomas Sandell
Made by ASPLUND
www.asplund.org

CAPO D'ORO
Designed by Paolo Pallucco & Mireille Rivier
Made by DE PADOVA
www.depadova.it

A set of hinges, with three trapezial tops, make this table capable of creating different shapes. Square when closed, upon turning the elements, the table opens up, composing different shapes until a trapezial top is achieved. Base consists of three white or aluminium powder coated structures with steel profiles. Hinges in stainless steel. Tops: in plywood veneered in white or aluminium laminate, flush with structure. Adjustable feet.

De Padova nos presenta esta original mesa con una estructura modular. Una serie de visagras trapezoidales permiten que la mesa adopte diversas formas. Su forma es cuadrada cuando está cerrada, pero al girar las partes que la componen podemos abrirla creando distintas formas. La base ha sido fabricada en aluminio en polvo con los perfiles de acero. Las visagras son de acero inoxidable. El tablero es de láminas de contrachapado de color blanco. Las patas son ajustables.

COMPAS
Designed by Jean Prouvé
Made by Vitra
www.vitra.com

COMPAS Table is a further exampleof Prouvé´s brilliance as a designer. Around 1950 he came up with this table frame with its slim metal legs that are formally reminiscent of the two point of a compass, in french, "le compas".

La COMPAS Table es un ejemplo más de la genialidad de Prouvé como diseñador. Hacia el año 1950, desarrolló este bastidor de mesa con esbeltas patas de metal, cuyas formas recuerdan a las dos agujas de un compás, en francés "le compas".

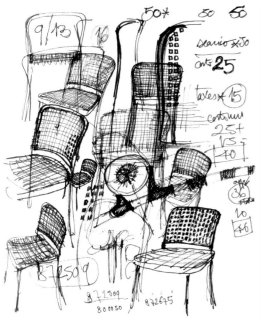

SILVER
Designed by Vico Magistretti
Made by DE PADOVA
www.depadova.it

Sitting system. Aluminium alloy structure. Seat and back in black, white, warm grey, grey, orange or cobalt blue polypropylene. Available, upon request, with special treatment for outdoor use. Seat cushion in expanded polyurethane with grey or ecrù cotton fabric cover which can be removed for dry cleaning. The cushion is attached to the polypropylene seat by means of snaps.

Sistema de asientos con estructura de aluminio. El respaldo y el asiento pueden ser en color blanco, negro, gris, naranja y azul cobalto y ha sido fabricado con polipropileno. También puede utilizarse en exteriores. Los cojines para el asiento son de poliuretano expandido con fundas de algodón en color gris y se limpian en seco. El cojín se sujeta al asiento mediante broches a presión.

WIRE CHAIR
Designed by Charles & Ray Eames
Made by VITRA
www.vitra.com

The Eames Wire Chair is a variation on the organically sha-ped one-piece seat shell, boasting a light transparency and high technicality. The chairs are available without upholstery, or with a single seat cushion or a seat and backrest cushion. Because of its shape, this upholstery is sometimes referred to as a "bikini".

Con la Wire Chair, los Eames varían el tema de la carcasa de asiento orgánica de una sola pieza, dándole una ligera transparencia y un alto grado de tecnicidad. Las sillas están disponibles sin tapizar, con cojines de asiento o con acolcha-dos para el asiento y el respaldo. En esta última versión, las sillas también se denominan "Bikini" debido a su forma.

EA 105 - EA 108
Designed by Charles & Ray Eames
Made by VITRA
www.vitra.com

The chairs in the Aluminium Group are the most famous creations by Charles and Ray Eames. Designed in 1958 they rate amongst the great achievements in the design history of the 20th century.

Las sillas de de aluminio de la colección Vitra son las creaciones más famosas de Charles Ray Eames. Diseñadas en 1958 son una de las mejores aportaciones al mundo del diseño de mobiliario del siglo veinte.

PSCC
Designed by Charles & Ray Eames
Made by VITRA
www.vitra.com

PSCC transforms the Side Chair into a swivelling office chair. In the current polypropylene version the Side Chair provides even greater.

PSCC transforma la Side Chair en una indispensable silla de oficina. En la versión actual en polipropileno la Side Chair es aún mucho mas duradera y resistente.

APILA
Designed by Carles Riart
Made by TRAMO
www.tramo.com

APILA is a new stacking system, which provided containers closed by doors with metallic supports and tops, bookcases with sliding doors, open elements, 45 cm deep wooden drawers and base-boards studied to connect all the other elements. There are two important compositions: the first one providing a solution as bookcase or tv set holder. The second one creates a very well equipped work area.

Ahora el sistema APILA crece mediante la posibilidad la incorporación de dos nuevos elementos : Un cajón en los módulos de 45 cm de profundidad que es de madera y los frontales acabados en melamina roble o wengué o lacados en blanco. Dobles puertas correderas que permiten cerrar completamente tanto los módulos de 90 cm como los de 180 cml. Los elementos que lo componen se ensamblan mediante un perfil de aluminio anodizado de forma ondulada, que dota a la pieza de una solidez sin utilizar ni un solo tornillo.

BLACK BETTY
Designed by Filippo Dell'Orto
Made by SPHAUS
www.sphaus.com

Chair with steel legs and hard polyurethane shell, lacquered with scratchproof embossed paint in the same colour (red, black or white). Seat upholstered with fabrics and leathers in catalogue.

Silla con patas de acero. Asiento y respaldo de una solo pieza realizado en poliuretano muy resistente con recubrimiento a prueba de arañazos en el mismo color. Se presentan en tapizados de distintas clases de tejidos o cueros.

TX
Designed by Estudi Disseny Blanc
Made by TRAMO.
www.tramo.com

The rigorous design of this stylized matt nickel steel structure turns it into a subtle but functional sculpture. The usual awkwardness of the legs is minimized, as they cross at their centre of gravity, giving the table its name: X.

El diseño riguroso de esta estilizada estructura de acero de níquel mate lo convierte en una escultura sutil pero funcional. La incomodidad habitual de las patas ha sido minimizada, ya que se cruzan en su centro de gravedad, dando a la mesa el evidente nombre de X.

OVAL
Designed by Estudi Blanc
Made by TRAMO
www.tramo.com

The versatility of OVAL resides in the installation possibilities because of the different ways of subjection and the possibility to adjust easyly any height or angle, which makes it very suitable for multiple spaces, from the home office, a design studio, to an exhibition fair.

La versatilidad de OVAL reside en sus posibilidades de instalación gracias a sus distintos sistemas de sujeción y a que se puede regular fácilmente a cualquier altura y con cualquier ángulo, por lo que puede instalarse en múltiples espacios, desde el despacho en casa, un estudio, zona de consulta o de exposición.

TORO
Designed by Bror Boije
Made by SWEDESE
www.swedese.se

Beautiful armchair designed by Brore Boije for Swedese, with adjustable back position and adjustable headrest.

Precioso sillón diseñado por Brore Boije para Swedese, con respaldo y reposa cabeza ajustables.

TWIST EASY CHAIR
Designed by Jerker Andersson
Made by SWEDESE
www.swedese.se

By the hand of designer Jerker Andersson, Swedese introduces us a swivel and amazing armchair with rocking mechanism.

De la mano del diseñador Jerker Andersson, la firma Swedese nos presenta esta maravillosa silla provista de un mecanismo que le permite balancearse.

ORGANIC CHAIR
Designed by Charles Eames & Eero Saarinen
Made by VITRA
www.vitra.com

The ORGANIC CHAIR is a comfortable small reading chair and was made in 1940 as a contribution to the New York MoMA's "Organic Design in Home Furnishings" competition. Formally speaking it was ahead of its time, but owing to the lack of manufacturing techniques, never went into series production. It was not until after 1950 that it became possible to manufacture larger quantities of organically shaped seat shells and market them. The first were chairs such as Eames' famous Plastic Armchair or Saarinen's Tulip Chair. Collection Vitra Design Museum.

La ORGANIC CHAIR es una pequeña pero cómoda silla perfecta para la lectura, fue diseñada en 1940 como contribución al concurso "Organic Design in Home Furnishings" para el MoMA (museo de arte contemporáneo de Nueva York). Adelantada en su tiempo nunca fué fabricada hasta que a finales de los años cincuenta fué posible su industrialización. Las primeras que se realizaron fueron fabricadas en plástico como la famosa silla diseñada por Eames PLASTIC ARMCHAIR o la TULIP CHAIR de Saarinen. Colección Vitra Design Museum.

A 660
Designed by James Irvine
Made by THONET
www.thonet.de

This beautiful office chair designed by James Irvine for Thonet is a bentwodd chair with round base (or crass legs) aluminium polished, turnable, plastic mesh in black, havanna or silver.

Silla de oficina diseñada por James Irvine para Thonet con estructura de madera, con con patas de aluminio pulido, el respaldo y el asiento se han solucionado con una malla plástica en diversos colores.

GIGI STACKING CHAIR
Designed by Marco Maran
Made by KNOLL
www.knoll.com

An ideal option for cafeterias, breakout rooms, auditoriums and training rooms and of course for home offices. Back flexes for comfort. Available with or without arms. Upholstered seat version with or without stacking bumper available on GIGI armless chair. Seat cushion secures to chair; seat cushion is not retrofittable. Unupholstered version stacks four to six chairs high on floor; can stack up to 12 chairs high on dolly with stacking bumper. Upholstered version stacks four chairs high on the floor and 10 chairs high on dolly. Accessories include ganging mechanism and tablet arm. Collection includes accessories, barstool, swivel chair and seat cushion.

GIGI es una opción ideal para la oficina en casa. Con respaldo flexible esta silla ha sido diseñada para dar el máximo comfort a los usuarios que se pasan la mayor parte del día trabajando sentados. Está disponible con o sin brazos y se pueden apilar un número aproximado de diez o doce sillas. Como accesorios tenemos una pequeña mesita de fácil mecanismo para montar en el brazo que hará las veces de pequeño escritorio y un cojín para el asiento forrado en una gran variedad de tejidos.

MOTHER
Designed by Filippo Dell'Orto
Made by SPHAUS
www.sphaus.com

Chair made by combining matt lacquered MDF and powder-coated aluminium in the same RAL colours so as to obtain consistency and continuity between the two materials, while at the same time underlining their differences.

Silla fabricada mediante la combinación de MDF mate lacado y polvo de aluminio en los mismos RAL colores, obteniendo una consistencia y continuidad entre los dos materiales, aunque al mismo tiempo destaquen sus diferencias.

LUNUGANGA
Designed by Cross/Mathias
Made by WOK
www.wokmedia.com

The piece is a response to the flooded, jungley environ-ment in which the designers were suddenly thrown into when they went to work in Sri Lanka. They wanted to take something of the feeling of the flooded environment home, a seed of the jungle to plant in your house which might invade it and take over. They took the image of partially submerged trees and translated it into shelves that have both the qualities of the overgrown lake that surrounded them and the quietness of European furniture.

La inspiración de esta pieza es la jungla inundada de Sri Lanka, lugar en el que estuvieron los diseñadores durante una temporada de trabajo. Querían trasladar ese ambiente de selva inundada a un espacio doméstico, como una especie de semilla. Tomaron la imagen de los árboles parcialmente sumergidos y lo tradujeron en estanterías, rompiendo con la sobriedad del diseño de mobiliario europeo.

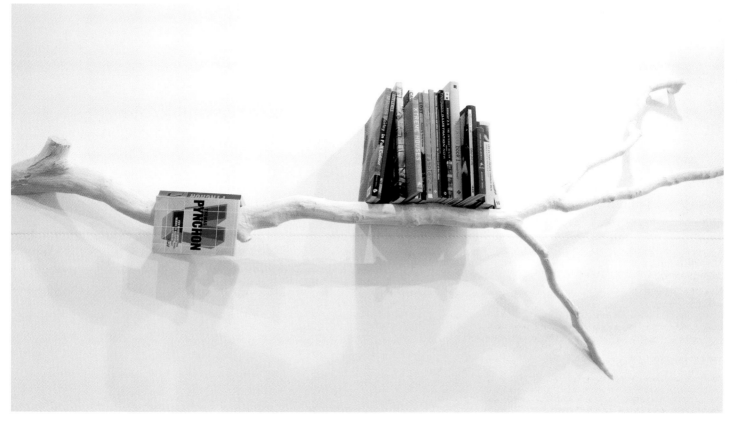

SYSTEM#1
Designed by Matali Crasset
Made by FREDRIKSON STALLARD

www.fredriksonstallard.com

Another amazing and minimalist shelving system. You can create it yourself
and extend it as much as you want.

Otro maravilloso y original diseño de estanterías. Tú mismo puedes crear esta
original estantería, y ampliarla cuanto quieras.

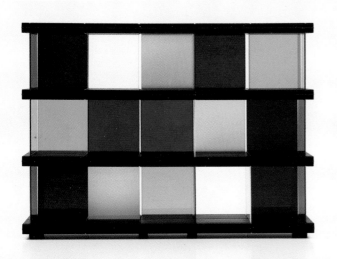

SELF
Designed by Ronan & Erwan Bouroullec
Made by VITRA
www.vitra.com

SELF is a modular shelved display cabinet which invites its user to interact with it. There are only two elements to Self. Its horizontal shelves and vertical dividing walls come in a variety of sizes and colours and can easily be built in flexible configurations and without tools. Self can be closed, open or accessed from both sides and can function as a bookshelf, display cabinet or room divider.
Material: Bases made of blown polypropylene, dividing walls of polycarbonate, pull rods of galvanized steel.

SELF es una vitrina de estantes modulares que anima al usuario a establecer una interacción. Se compone de sólo dos módulos: las baldas horizontales y las paredes de separación verticales se pueden combinar fácilmente en incontables tamaños y variantes de color sin necesidad de utilizar herramienta alguna. Así, se crean Selfs cerrados, abiertos o accesibles por ambos lados, que se pueden utilizar como estantería para libros, vitrina o separador de ambientes.

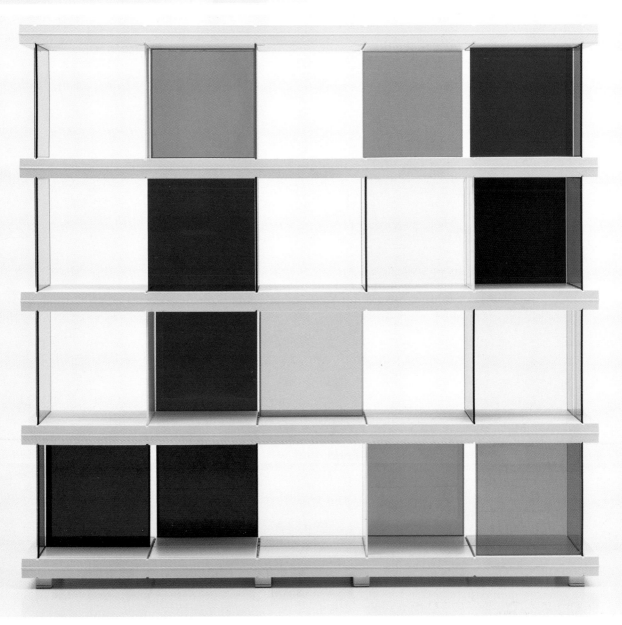

TRACE
Designed by Desalto
Made by AZUMI
www.azumi.co.uk

This is a small, wrap-around armchair, made of engineering polymer Hyrek. The shape came from a traced outline of an armchair - in other words, the lines are picked up from the afterimage of a typical armchair which is exposed into your retina.
Shell: Hyrek (Engineering polymer)
Legs: Stainless steel legs

Diseñado por Desalto para Azumi, esta silla ha sido creada a imagen y semejanza del típico sillón tal y como se queda grabada en nuestra retina. El asiento está hecho con polímero Hyrek y las patas son de acero inoxidable.

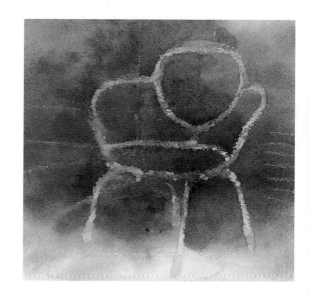

TWO TOPS
Designed by Marcel Wanders
Made by MOOOI
www.moooi.com

Designer Marcel Wanders says: "I made a mistake, I fixed the table-top under the supporting bars instead of on top, and found a space which was always there but was never seen, I created a lid to cover and to hide and change a few hundred years of classic table-making".
Materials: oak frame, MDF with oak veneer top.

El diseñador Marcel Wanders creó esta espectacular mesa de oficina a partir de un error que cometió montando una mesa dejando un espacio entre el tablero y las barras de soporte. Con ese concepto ideó una tapa que escondía el espacio diseñado para el escritorio. Muy funcional este escritorio o mesa de trabajo se puede convertir con facilidad en una improvisada mesa para reuniones. Toda la mesa está fabricada en madera de roble.

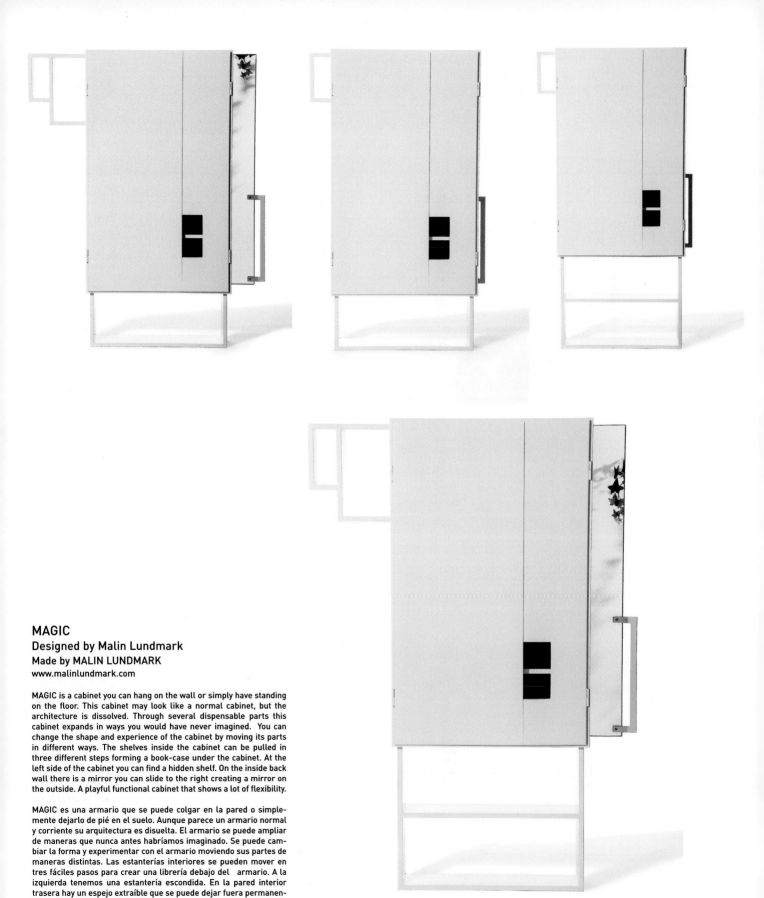

MAGIC
Designed by Malin Lundmark
Made by MALIN LUNDMARK
www.malinlundmark.com

MAGIC is a cabinet you can hang on the wall or simply have standing on the floor. This cabinet may look like a normal cabinet, but the architecture is dissolved. Through several dispensable parts this cabinet expands in ways you would have never imagined. You can change the shape and experience of the cabinet by moving its parts in different ways. The shelves inside the cabinet can be pulled in three different steps forming a book-case under the cabinet. At the left side of the cabinet you can find a hidden shelf. On the inside back wall there is a mirror you can slide to the right creating a mirror on the outside. A playful functional cabinet that shows a lot of flexibility.

MAGIC es una armario que se puede colgar en la pared o simple-mente dejarlo de pié en el suelo. Aunque parece un armario normal y corriente su arquitectura es disuelta. El armario se puede ampliar de maneras que nunca antes habríamos imaginado. Se puede cam-biar la forma y experimentar con el armario moviendo sus partes de maneras distintas. Las estanterías interiores se pueden mover en tres fáciles pasos para crear una librería debajo del armario. A la izquierda tenemos una estantería escondida. En la pared interior trasera hay un espejo extraíble que se puede dejar fuera permanen-temente u ocultar según nos interese.

SQ3
Designed by Alessandra Bettolo & Betty Sperandeo
Made by SPHAUS
www.sphaus.com

Shelves sold in single columns available in two heights (254/192 cm) with a depth of 30cm. The taller column comes with three cubes of coloured methacrylate, while the shorter version has two.
Available finishes: white plastic laminate or lacquered with matt polyurethane paint in the colours shown in the catalogue.

Sphaus nos presenta estas estanterías que se venden por columnas separadas y disponibles en dos medidas (254/192 cm) con una profundidad de 30 cm. La columna mas alta viene con tres cubos de metacrilato coloreado, mientras que la más pequeña tiene dos.

DES USINES
Designed by Bouroullec
Made by VITRA

www.bouroullec.com
www.vitra.com

Bouroullec started his collaboration with Vitra in January 2001. Since that date he has created and designed several pieces and solutions for office room's furniture. On these pages you could see some samples of these amazing collaboration.

Bouroullec empezó a colaborar con Vitra en Enero del 2001. Desde esa fecha ha creado y diseñado una infinidad de mobiliario específico para oficinas. En estas páginas encontramos algunos ejemplos de esa maravillosa colaboración.

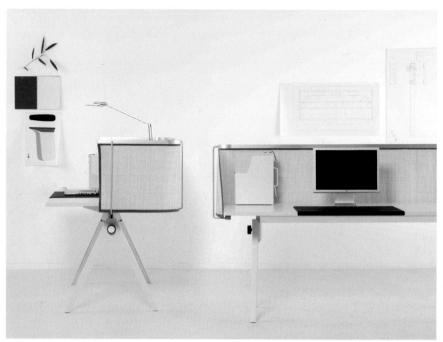

TOWERS

Designed by Knoll

Made by KNOLL

www.knoll.com

Well-built Rugged. Diverse. Knoll storage towers offer design flexibility, personalizing workspaces with style.

De Construcción sólida Rugosa. Diverso. Las torres de almacenaje de Knoll ofrecen flexibilidad de diseño, personalizando las zonas de trabajo con estilo.

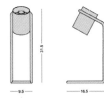

MINI-ME

Designed by Filipo Gordon Frank

Made by SPHAUS

www.sphaus.com

Table light lacquered with matt anti-scratch paint.

Lámpara de mesa lacada con pintura mate antirasguños.

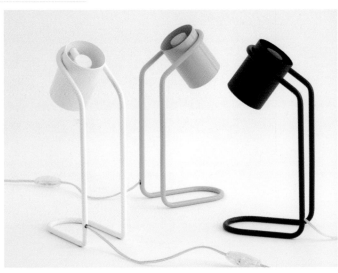

Five shelves are rebated with two slots on 45 degree angles. These slots align with the horizontal rails on two fabricated ladder frames. When the shelves are fitted with these frames it creates a 3 dimensional rhombus form that is self-structural . Assembly requires no tools and no screws, glues or connectors . SOL does not require cross bracing rods and therefore the five shelves appear to balance from the vertical stems. Sol shelving is dedicated to one of Didier's favourite sculptors: Sol LeWitt .

De la mano del diseñadro Ross Didier nos llega la estantería SOL. Su montaje es tan sencillo que no precisa de la ayuda de ninguna herramienta, tornillos, pegamento o clavos. De aspecto limpio y moderno SOL está dedicada por Didier a su escultor favorito: Sol LeWitt.

BAHUT
Designed by Jean Prouvé
Made by VITRA
www.vitra.com

In his furniture designs, Jean Prouvé combines his technical know-how and the opportunities offered by his production facility in Maxéville with his unique industrial aesthetics. The BAHUT sideboard dating from 1951 has an unusual decorative character thanks to the use of diamond sheet metal, emphasized by the cream-white lacquer.
Materials: folded sheet aluminium and steel, suspended doors made of diamond-shaped plate, handles of solid oak.

Para sus diseños de mobiliario, Jean Prouvé combina sus amplios conocimientos técnicos con su gran sensibilidad de la estética. El BAHUT es un mueble que se creó en los años cincuenta con carácter decorativo gracias al uso del metal laminado en forma de diamantes, enfatizado con un lacado color nata.
Materiales: aluminio y acero, puertas laminadas con metal en forma de diamantes y tiradores de roble.

please, do not disturb!

porfavor, no molestar

Aside from the personal hygiene aspect we shouldn't forget that there are also great rewards to be had from taking a bath after an exhausting day at work, a long journey or after practicing sport.
In short, when we speak of the bathroom, we are referring to far more just than its role as regards our personal hygiene, we are also referring to what we perceive to be an oasis in the midst of a frantic modern lifestyle, a place to relax and be lost in rejuvenating thought.
The following designs are a faithful reflection of present day needs in this particular room of the house.

Además de las funciones de higiene personal, no debemos olvidar que el baño puede aportarnos una serie de compensaciones tras una agotadora jornada, un largo viaje o después de la práctica de un deporte.
En definitiva, cuando hablamos de funciones propias del cuarto de baño, nos estamos refiriendo a mucho más que a las meras funciones higiénicas, estamos refiriéndonos también a ese oasis que, en la agitada vida moderna, significa relax y recreación contemplativa.
Los diseños que se exponen a continuación son fiel reflejo de las necesidades actuales en estos espacios de la casa.

On the following pages bathroom designed by Jaime Hayon
En las páginas siguients baño diseñado por Jaime Hayon

AERI EVOLUTION
Designed by Altro
Made by ALTRO
www.altro.es

Designed by Altro, the wooden pieces in this collection have a hallmark all of their own, made as they are from curved plywood sheets. Also unusual is the fact that the back of the doors have been covered with a magnetic plate to which various accessories can be attached or alternatively be used as a prop for photographs or notes, etc.

Las piezas en madera tienen como sello particular de esta colección, diseñada por Altro, la elaboración con tablero contrachapado curvado. Así mismo destaca la particularidad que la parte interior de las puertas se ha revestido con una plancha magnética a la que se pueden adherir diferentes complementos o bien utilizarla como soporte para fotografías, notas, etc.

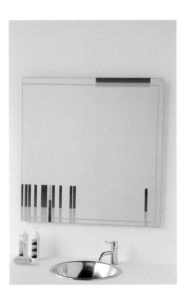 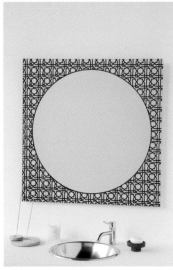 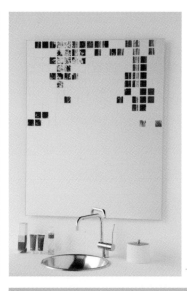 

From top left to right
De izquierda a derecha
IDEX, TANGER, LOST, BONTH & DIVINE
Designed by Jose Manuel Ferrero
Made by ESTUDI HAC
www.estudihac.com

Designer Jose Manuel Ferrero delights us with his collection of mirrors which have been screen printed with a variety of motifs, created exclusively for ESTUDI HAC.

El diseñador Jose Manuel Ferrero nos deleita con esta exquisite colección de espejos serigrafiados con distintos motivos, creados exclusivamente para la firma ESTUDI HAC.

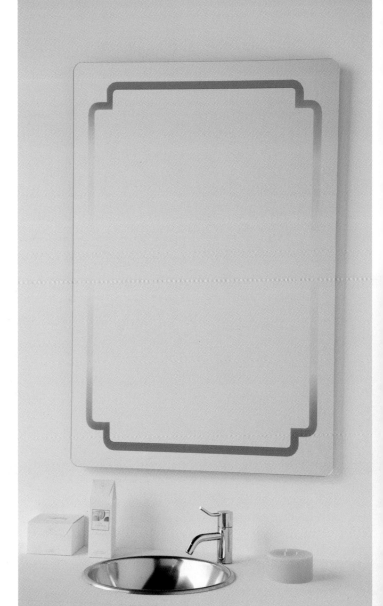

ELEGANT
Designed by Jaime Hayon
Made by ArtQuitect
www.hayonstudio.com
www.artquitect.net

The bathroom collection, designed by Jaime Hayon for ArtQuitect, has been extended with the addition of new items: a marvellous bath with a variety of accessories to customise it, a multi-purpose glazed cabinet and a series of glass and ceramic containers.

La colección de baño que Jaime Hayon ha diseñado para ArtQuitect se amplía con nuevos elementos. Una bañera maravillosa con diversos accesorios para personalizarla, un mueble-vitrina multiuso y una serie de contenedores en cerámica y cristal.

BRILLANT
Designed by Jaime Hayon
Made by ArtQuitect
www.hayonstudio.com
www.artquitect.net

Chic and sophisticated. Brilliant in their conception and in their making. In stylised shapes and Baroque silhouettes, Hayón draws inspiration from the quality of the materials and the aesthetic of another time, but uses the technology of today to develop them and puts all his ingenuity into recreating them.

Chic y sofisticado. Brillante en su concepción y también en la realización. Hayon se inspira en calidad de los materiales y en la estética de otro tiempo, en las formas estilizadas y las siluetas barrocas, pero usa la tecnología de hoy para desarrollarlas y pone el ingenio para recrearlas.

ELEGANT
Designed by Jaime Hayon
Made by ArtQuitect
www.hayonstudio.com
www.artquitect.net

A return to elegant bathrooms, like the ones of years ago, when they represented social status in the home or in a restaurant. A return to the past with an eye on the future. To recover the distinction of beautiful objects in our time.

La vuelta a los baños elegantes, como los de antaño, cuando eran espacios que representaban el estatus social en la casa o en el restaurante. Un retorno al pasado mirando al futuro. Para recuperar en nuestro tiempo la prestancia de los objetos bellos.

TWIN
Designed by Altro
Made by ALTRO
www.altro.es

Altro brings us a delightful collection which comprises a vanity top and lower shelf in different coloured laminated glass in. Both are custom made, which also includes customising the colour combination to add an avant-garde touch to the sobriety of the bathroom.

Altro nos presenta un delicioso conjunto compuesto por encimera y repisa inferior de vidrio laminado en distintos colores. Ambos se fabrican a medida siendo posible también la combinación de colores aportando un toque de vanguardia a la sobriedad del cuarto de baño.

HAPPY D
Designed by Sieger Design & Duravit
Made by DURAVIT
www.duravit.es

This collection of bathroom furniture from Duvarit is of pure and simple lines and a very practical design, the perfect solution for smaller bathrooms. The collection includes modular units and occasional pieces with wheels, mirrors and mirrored wall units, washbasin stands available in different widths which are complemented by cabinets with curved doors.

Duvarit nos presenta una colección de muebles de baño con un diseño puro y muy funcional ideal para baños de espacio reducido. La colección incluye muebles modulares y auxiliares con ruedas, espejos y armarios de espejo, muebles lavabo de distintos anchos que se complementan con muebles de puertas curvadas.

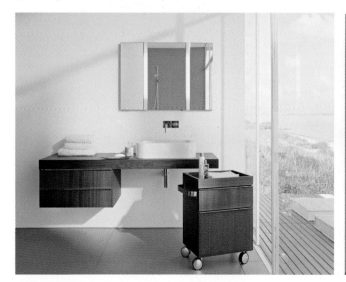

AERI-PROJECT
Designed by Estudio Roviras & Torrente Ass
Made by ALTRO
www.altro.es

This striking minimalist monoblock sink comes from the Aeri collection by Altro. Manufactured in stainless steel, the sink, mirror, lighting, electronic photocell operated taps and soap dispenser are all incorporated within one single element. This original collection also includes a stainless steel photocell controlled urinal as well as a wall mounted toilet bowl with a built-in cistern.

La colección Aeri de Altro nos presenta un llamativo lavabo monoblock de carácter minimalista. Fabricado en acero inoxidable incorpora en un sólo elemente el lavabo, espejo, iluminación, grifería electrónica con fotocélula y dispensador de jabón. Dentro de esta original colección encontramos un urinario tambien en acero inoxidable y fotocélula, además de un inodoro para montaje mural con cisterna empotrada.

KNOT
Designed by Julie Mathias
Made by WOK media
www.wokmedia.com

We wondered what happened inside, inside your stomach, inside the toilet, inside the sewer.....Did you ever sit on a toilet resting or hiding, and asking yourself, where does it go? However did I get here? Knot Toilette asks all those questions with you, it's all about digestion. We decided to show the contorted pipes which are often hidden inside   toilets, to uncover them, twist them even more and propose a different kind of aesthetic for toilets, based not on concealing but showing.

Nos preguntamos lo que pasó dentro, dentro de tu estómago, dentro de los servicios, dentro de la alcantarilla...¿Te has sentado algunad vez en un descanso de servicios, oculto, preguntándote a ti mismo, a dónde va? El "Knot Toilette" (taza nudo) se hace todas esas preguntas dobre la digestión. Julie Mathias decidió con este diseño mostrar los tubos torcidos que no vemos en los servicios para destaparlos y enroscarlos hasta conseguir una estética diferente para el diseño del cuarto de baño.

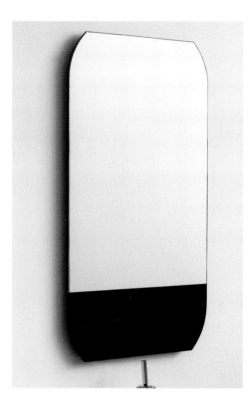

MANIAQUA
Designed by Equipo técnico Altro
Made by ALTRO
www.altro.es

The latest addition to the well known Aqua collection from Altro is MiniAqua, the new smaller sized version of a vanity top complete with hand basin and integrated towel rail, available in two transparent glass finishes or blue laminated, the towel rails are chromium plated brass and the hand basin stainless steel.
Dimensions : 550 x 360 x 850 mm

La más reciente versión de la conocida colección Aqua de Altro, es el nuevo MiniAqua, una variante que presenta en unas dimensiones mínimas una encimera con lavabo y soporte con toallero integrado, se realiza en dos acabados de cristal transparente o laminado azul, los soportes son de latón cromado y el lavabo de acero inoxidable.
D i m e n s i o n e s : 550 x 360 x 850 mm

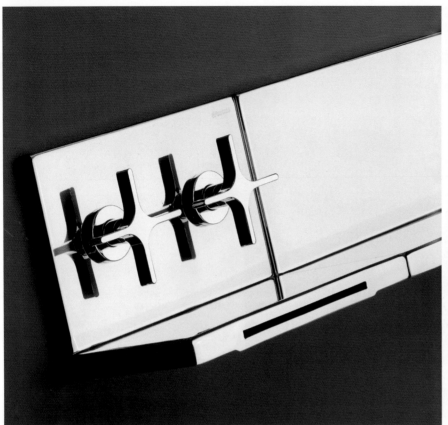

WATERBLADE
Designed by Peter Jamieson
Made by RITMONIO
www.ritmonio.it

Clear and sharp, WATERBLADE is a modular system of shelves that exalts the most natural movement of the water: the waterfall. However a controlled movement, a blade, a sweet blade, that is broken against your hands.

El sistema de grifo y estantería modular WATERBLADE exalta el movimiento más natrual del agua: La cascada.
El movimiento controlado del agua hace que ésta caiga suavemente sobre las manos.

AERI VETRO
Designed by Altro
Made by ALTRO
www.altro.es

The new AERI bathroom collection bring us the latest curve crystal stucking technology, the union between the different surfaces that shape the piece represents the perfect combination between skill and craft. The obtained product is one of a kind.

Los nuevos lavabos de la colección AERI incorporan la última tecnología en curvado y encolado de vidrio, la unión entre las diferentes superficies que conforman el lavabo representa la perfecta combinación entre técnica y artesanía. El producto obtenido es de una sutileza y calidad formal fuera de lo común.

HAPPY D
Designed by Sieger Design & Duravit
Made by DURAVIT
www.duravit.es

Anyone seeking to relax at the end of a stressful day will find just that in HAPPY D, in the form of a comfortable whirlpool bath complete with air and a pleasant multicoloured lighting system. All items in the range bring to mind the distinctive shape of the letter D - and are a real lucky strike when it comes to form, function and affordability. Sometimes one letter is all it takes to open up a new bathroom world. And bring a smile to your face.

Para los que buscan relajamiento al final de un día estresante encontrarán en el HAPPY D una confortable bañera de hidromasaje con sistema de aire y una agradable luz multicolor.
Todos los productos de la serie HAPPY D tienen como común denominador, que han sido diseñados inspirados en la forma de la letra D.

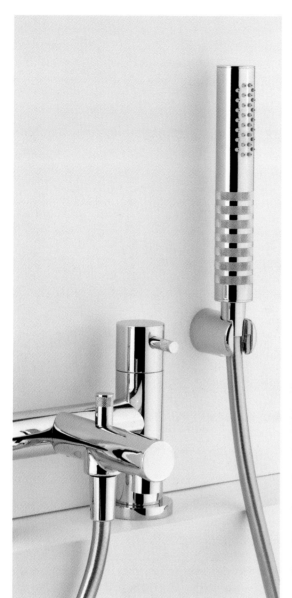

DIAMETROTRENTACINQUE
Designed by Davide Vercelli
Made by RITMONIO
www.ritmonio.it

A diameter of 35mm is an ergonomically correct measurment. A long process of elimination to reach the point where there are only essential lines. It is through this interpenetration of pure volumes that the advanced technology of a compact cartridge assures the right flow to remind us that the water is a precious element.

Un diámetro de 35mm es una medida ergonómica ideal. Tras un largo proceso de eliminación Davide Vercelli alcanzó el punto en el que sólo existen líneas esenciales. Es gracias a esta interpretación de volúmenes puros que la tecnología avanzada de un cartucho compacto garantiza el flujo correcto recordándonos que el agua es un elemento precioso.

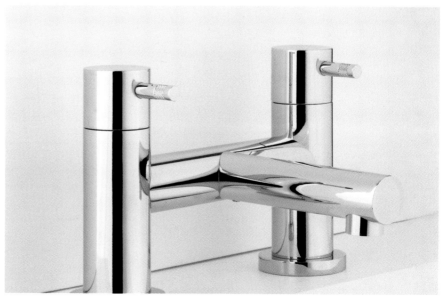

BRIDGE
Designed by Flaminia
Made by COMSA
www.comercialsanitaria.com

Simplicidad y funcionalidad distinguen el mueble BRIDGE; el cual concede el máximo protagonismo a la calidad de los materiales y a las formas. Disponible a partir de 90 cm y hasta 2 metros de largo y en acabados de madera lacada, roble, wengué y zebrano.
Dimensiones: A partir de 70 cm a 2 metros de largo x 80 cm de alto x 55 cm de ancho

Simplicity and practicality are the keys to the BRIDGE furniture, maximum importance having been placed upon the quality of the materials and the design. Available in lengths from 90cm up to 2 metres and in a choice of lacquered wood finishes, oak, wenge and zebrano.
Dimensions: From 70 cm to 2 metres long x 80 cm height x 55 cm width.

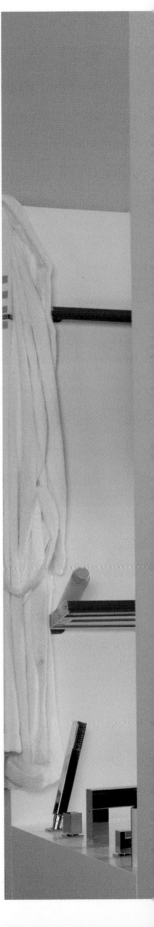

ANTONIO MIRO BAÑO
Designed by Antonio Miró
Made by ALTRO
www.altro.es

The Antonio Miró Bath collection from ALTRO comprises all the usual bathroom basics and logically displays this designer's answer to bathroom furniture, accessories and complements. The usual sobriety of Miro's design and his personality is undoubtedly conveyed in these bathroom products, the quality of materials and technical developments all of which demonstrate the intensity of professional involvement which includes technical and developmental support from New York architect Lucho Marcial and Altro's own Technical Team.

La colección Antonio Miró Baño de ALTRO comprende los elementos básicos de un cuarto de baño, y presenta de manera racional las soluciones del diseñador en mobiliario de baño, accesorios y complementos. La sobriedad habitual del diseño de Miró y su personalidad se trasmiten de manera indudable a los productos de baño, la calidad de los materiales y el desarrollo técnico muestran la profundidad de un trabajo profesional que ha contado con la participación del arquitecto neoyorquino Lucho Marcial y del Equipo de Altro, como soporte técnico y de desarrollo.

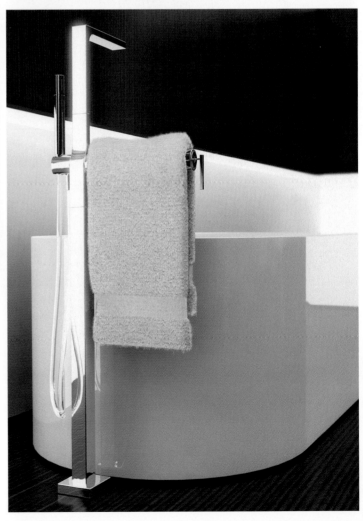

WATERBLADE_J
Designed by Peter Jamieson
Made by RITMONIO
www.ritmonio.it

WATERBLADE_J, coming from the natural growth of the Waterblade series, develops with autonomy and its own identity. The rectangular section and the importance of the proportions are the formal characteristics, completed by the comfort of the mixer and the lightness of the joystick handle.

El WATERBLAD_J, está diseñado con autonomía e identidad propia. La sección rectangular y la importancia de las proporciones son sus características formales, completado con un cómodo mezclador de agua y la ligereza de su palanca de mando.

in my secret garden

en mi jardín secreto

A great deal is spoken about the soul of objects, their powers of seduction and of the human being's obsession with attaching itself not only to other human beings but also inert elements such as a chest of drawers, a chair, a teaspoon or a sofa. For this reason the home becomes our safe haven, the one place we can truly relax and feel most at ease.

And for those which have a garden, this becomes the principal relaxation zone, weather permitting that is. For this very reason, that is the pleasure of taking a well earned rest, garden furniture now combines materials such as teak and fabric, beech wood and aluminium, batyline, wrought iron or wicker.... The frontier between indoor and outdoor furniture has virtually disappeared, materials are becoming lighter, designs are just as appealing indoors as outdoors, garden furniture is now designed to be more comfortable, the styles are more refined and the finishes better. Appearance, textures, colours and scents all adopt great importance when it comes to having an influence on the users mind and these are the very elements the designer plays with in order to promote the attachment of which we spoke earlier.

Se habla mucho del alma de los objetos, de su poder de seducción y de la manía del ser humano de apegarse no solo a otros seres, sino también a elementos inertes como una cómoda, una silla, una cucharilla o un sofá. Por eso la casa se alza como el refugio cálido y formal en el que nos sentimos más a gusto, nuestro lugar de descanso. Y para aquellas que disponen de jardín, éste se convierte, en el principal lugar de descanso cuando las condiciones meteorológicas lo permiten. Es por este motivo, el placer del descanso, que el mobiliario de jardín mezcla las materias de teca y tejido, de haya y aluminio, de batilina, de forja o de mimbre... La frontera entre el mobiliario interior y exterior está desapareciendo, las materias son cada vez más ligeras, las creaciones son tan bellas dentro como fuera, las formas del mobiliario de jardín se hacen más confortables, las líneas más refinadas, los acabados más cuidados. La apariencia, las texturas, los colores, los aromas, toman gran importancia a la hora de influir en la psicología del usuario y son los elementos con los que el diseñador juega para conseguir esa atracción que previamente comentábamos.

On the following pages furniture designed by Triconfort.
En las páginas siguientes mobiliario diseñado por Triconfort.

VIA
Designed by Kettal
Made by KETTAL
www.kettalgroup.com

Kettal is a delight to our eyes with this stupendous collection of outdoor furniture. Particularly remarkable are the stackable aluminium sun-loungers with a polyester paint finish. Highly weather resistant and available in two different versions with interchangeable backs and seats, one version made with synthetic fibre and the other with Poretex.

Kettal nos regala la vista con esta estupenda colección de muebles para exteriores. Destacan las tumbonas amontonables entre sí realizadas en aluminio con acabados en pintura de poliéster. De gran resistencia al aire libre podemos encontrarlas en dos versiones con respaldo y asiento intercambiables, una versión fabricada con fibra sintética y otra realizada en Poretex.

BIARRITZ
Designed by Triconfort
Made by TRICONFORT
www.kettalgroup.com

The new collection Biarritz by Triconfort is made of aluminium and synthetic fiber. Acrylic fabric is UV stablised for colour fastness.

La nueva colección Biarritz de Triconfort ha sido realizada con aluminio y fibra artificial. El tejido utilizado es el Dralon con tratamiento anti-rayos UV, tratamiento antimoho y antimanchas, ideal para muebles de exterior.

Q STOOL
Designed by Danny Venlet
Made by VITEO
www.viteo.at

Originally conceived as a piece of indoor furniture, the Q Stool with its Outdoor Skai fittings (in white, cocoa, blue, lemon) and watertight seams is equally perfect for use in the open. The water-resistant interior foam and a stainless steel ring guarantee that even a sudden downpour will make no difference at all.
In the Q Stool, Danny Venlet has created something which has now developed far beyond what it was actually intended for. A foot stool, a doorstop, a plaything for children, or an umbrella stand for the hallway.
And as more and more people learn to love the form and function of the Q Stool, so more and more uses will be discovered as well.

Concebido originalmente como una pieza de mobiliario para interiores, el Q Stool está realizado con un skai especial para exteriores (en blanco, cacao, azul, limón) y resistente al agua, lo hace ideal para su uso en lugares al aire libre. La espuma interior también resistente al agua y un anillo de acero inóxidable garantizan que después de un chaparrón repentino lo mantenga intacto y en perfecto estado.
El diseñdor Danny Venlet ha creado algo más que un taburete, también se puede usar como reposa piés, un tope para puertas, un juguete para niños o un paragüero para el vestíbulo, etc...

BENCH AND TABLE
Designed by C.Bataille & P.Ibens
Made by FELD
www.feld.be

Bench & Table is a harmonious collection of different benches and a table. Responding to the needs of today this furniture fits almost in every interior, from classic to modern, from indoor to outdoor. The beauty lies in every detail. Back to basics. The collection is made out of wood for the indoor and the outdoor use, available in different lacquered colours. An oak varnished version is also available for the indoor and an un-treated afzelia version for the outdoor.

Bench & Table es una colección armoniosa de distintos bancos y una mesa. Respondiendo a las necesidades del mobiliario actual esta colección puede ajustarse a cualquier interior , desde los más clásicos a los modernos, y a cualquier exterior. La belleza está en cada pequeño detalle. La colección ha sido realizada en madera en diferentes colores laqueados.

OUTDOOR KITCHEN
Designed by Viteo
Made by VITEO
www.viteo.at

From Viteo, this original and practical outdoor kitchen turns any meal or dinner into an authentic open air celebration.

La firma Viteo nos presenta esta original y útil cocina para exteriores, convirtiendo las comidas o cenas en auténticas celebraciones al aire libre.

RIVAGE
Designed by Triconfort
Made by TRICONFORT
www.kettalgroup.com

Cutting-edge design for this outdoor furniture collection designed by the Triconfort team for Kettal. Made from high quality lacquered aluminium and different coloured Potorex.

Diseño y vanguardia para esta colección de muebles de exterior diseñada por el equipo de Triconfort para la firma Kettal. Fabricados en aluminio lacado de alta calidad y Potorex de distintos colores.

SOFT
Designed by Kettal
Made by KETTAL
www.kettalgroup.com

Stackable armchair designed by Kettal with structure in aluminium tubing finished with polyester paint, top quality teak and porotex very resistant to outdoors.

Sillones apilables de la firma Kettal con estructura realizada en tubo de aluminio pintado con polvo de poliéster, madera de teka y porotex, con chasis resistente a la intemperie.

SHOWER
Designed by Danny Venlet
Made by VITEO
www.viteo.at

All you need to do is step into the Viteo Shower. Your body weight sets off shower jets arranged in a circle around the edge of the foot panel. The jets first gush up and meet in the middle over your head before falling gently down like rain. To dispel the "cloud" and let the sun shine through once more you simply step off the foot panel. The white foot panel has a diameter of 80 cm and is made of UV resistant, non-slip plastic, with the substructure enclosed in a stainless steel ring. Water is supplied via a standard -inch garden hose with a "Gardena" connection. The height of the water column varies between two and four metres depending on the water pressure. The combination of white plastic and stainless steel conveys a visual impression of lightness to the Viteo Shower which finds its counterpart in the product's surprisingly low weight of around 14 kg.

Todo lo que necesitas es subirte encima de la Viteo Shower. El peso de nuestro propio cuerpo hará que los surtidores de alrededor de la plataforma de agua se pongan en funcionamiento. Los surtidores primero expulsa el agua a borbotones a una altura superior a nuestra cabeza cayendo después suave como la lluvia. Para que el agua deje de salir solo hay que volver a bajar de la plataforma. La plataforma, que tiene un diametro de 80 cm y pesa apróximadamente 14 kg, está hecha de plástico antideslizante y es muy resistente a los rayos ultravioleta. Para suministrar el agua es suficiente con conectar una simple manguera de jardín.

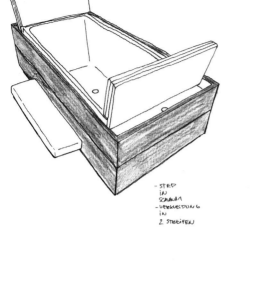

SUNDECK
Designed by EOOS group
Made by Duravit
www.duravit.com

Here. There. Everywhere. In the bathroom. In the living room. On the patio...Sundeck, the all-new bathtub by Duravit is a stroke of pure genius. In every respect and every setting. Created ba the EOOS group of designers, Sundeck makes a stunning impact with luxerious real wood panelling that can rope with any bathroom climate. But Sundeck has dreams to go beyond the bathroom. Its agreeable nature means that Sundeck is at ease anywhere in the home. Well, anywhere that's got running water. And, like a casket containing something precious, Sundeck can be sealed. Thanks to an ingenious cover designed to keep the fragrant bath water warm. But that's not all. When folded, the cover serves as a comfortable headrest. Opened out, it's a relaxing lounger - a veritable sundeck for well being worshippers. Sundeck brightens up a lot more than just the bathroom. Here. There. Everywhere.

Aquí. Allí. En todas partes. En el cuarto de baño. En la sala de estar. En el patio...Sundeck, la nueva bañera de Duravit, es un golpe de puro ingenio. Creado por los diseñadores EOOS group, Sundeck impacta por su lujosos paneles de madera natural que se aclimatan a cualquier cuarto de baño. Pero Sundeck se resiste a quedar encerrada entre las cuatro paredes de un cuarto de baño. Y, como un cofre que contiene algo precioso, la Sundeck puede cerrarse gracias a una ingeniosa cubierta diseñada para mantener el agua del baño caliente. Pero esto no es todo. Cuando se cierra, la cubierta se convierte en una cómoda camilla para estirarse y relajarse. Aquí. Allí. En todas partes.

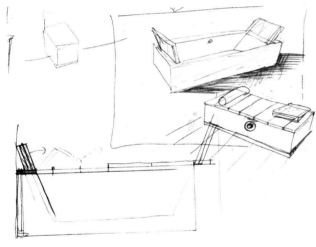

TUAREC
Designed by Viteo
Made by VITEO
www.viteo.at

What makes the TUAREC so outstanding is the smooth-running mechanism it employs to roll the awning up and out: this consists of a stainless steel handwheel with a diameter of 80 cm.

The idea that it's more pleasant to sit under a light-coloured sunshade than under a dark awning isn't true, either objectively or subjectively. On the contrary. The Tuareg, who lend their name to the new awnings from the VITEO_Fresh Designs series, have known this for centuries, and that's why the VITEO_Tuarec by Sunsquare® is not only available in silvery white, but also in a dark cloth with maximum light fastness, something which also makes this outdoor summer furniture both decorative and elegant at the same time.

Lo que hace tan excepcional al TUAREC es el suave mecanismo que emplea para enrollar el toldo impermeable, fabricado con acero inoxidable y con un diámetro de 80 cm. El concepto que tenemos de que es más agradable sentarse bajo una sombrilla de color claro que bajo un toldo de color oscuro no es verdadera, sino todo lo contrario. Los Tuareg, inspiración para toda la serie de diseños de VITEO, han sabido esto durante siglos, por eso el VITEO_Tuarec® no está sólo disponible en el típico blanco plateado, sino también en un tejido oscuro pero firme y ligero, algo que convierte este mobiliario de verano al aire libre en un objeto tanto decorativo como elegante a un mismo tiempo.

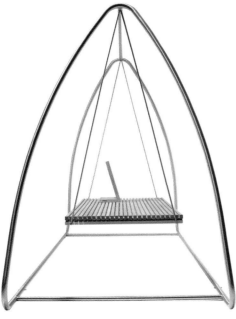

LIGHT CUBES & SWING
Designed by Viteo
Made by VITEO
www.viteo.at

It is the twilight hour. Darkness gradually falls and the noise of the day melts away into the peace of night-time. It is time to relax - with light sculptures from Viteo outdoors. The LIGHT CUBE and the SWING rocking bench have been specially designed for outdoor use and expand the range of moods for you to enjoy. These moments belong to you.

Ha llegado el atardecer. La oscuridad empieza a invadir el ambiente gradualmente y el ruido del día se mezcla con la noche. Es tiempo de relajarse con las esculturas luminiscentes de Viteo para exteriores. El LIGHT CUBE y el banco SWING han sido especialmente diseñados para su uso en exteriores.

ELYSEE
Designed by Triconfort
Made by TRICONFORT
www.kettalgroup.com

100% weatherproof!. Anti-static! (dust adheres less).
Anti UV! (it does not turn yellow). Very hard and solid.
Made with doublethickness Porotex which is available in
different colours (white, gray, yellow and blue).

¡100% impermeable!. ¡Antiestático! (el polvo se adhiere
menos). ¡Anti UVA! (no se volverá amarillo). Fuerte y
solido. Fabricado en porotex grueso y de doble espesor,
material disponible en diversos colores (blanco, gris,
amarillo y azul).

RIVIERA
Designed by Triconfort
Made by TRICONFORT
www.kettalgroup.com

Just a quick glance is enough to immediately transport to summertime thanks to this marine blue and white linear print, the perfect choice for this indispensable collection for any terrace or garden by the sea or pool.
Materials: lacquered resin, UV treated, mould and stain resistant DRALON fabric.

Simplemente hechándoles un vistazo nos transportan automáticamente al verano gracias a los colores del estampado lineal azul marino y blanco, muy acertados para esta colección indispensable en cualquier terraza o jardín cerca del mar o con piscina.
Materiales: resina lacada, tejido DRALON con tratamiento anti-rayos UV, tratamiento antimoho y antimanchas.

HI-POUFF
Designed by Matali Crasset
Made by DOMODINAMICA
www.domodinamica.com

Manufactured from aluminium profiles and painted with pow-
dered polyester paint. Remavable polyester vinyl fabric. This
collection allows one to choose a cross in another polyester
vinyl colour in the backs for all the models. If another colour is
not specified for the cross, the it will be manufactured in the
same chosen polyester vinyl colour. The tables are avaliable in
sanded or painted glass and in oil-treated teak for outdoors.

Colección fabricada en perfil de aluminio pintado con poliéster
en polvo. Asientos y respaldos en tejido de vinilo en poliéster
recambiable. Esta colección permite elegir una cruz en otro
color de vinilo poliéster en el respaldo de todos sus modelos, si
no se especifica otro color para la cruz, se confeccionará en el
mismo color del vinilo poliéster elegido. Las mesas están
diseñadas, en cristal arenado, pintado y en teka tratada con
aceite para el uso exterior.

XXL
Designed by Kettal
Made by KETTAL
www.kettalgroup.com

From Kettal comes a new collection of designer furniture for the terrace. Both the sofas and chairs and the rest of this modular collection are traditionally hand woven. The tubular aluminium structure is covered in a high quality synthetic fibre which like the frame is highly resistant to the elements.

Kettal nos presenta su nueva colección de muebles de diseño para terraza. Tanto los sofás como las sillas y el resto de la colección modular se presentan con un trenzado a mano artesanalmente. La estructura en tubo de aluminio recubierto con fibra sintética de gran calidad y resistencia como su chasis, resistente a la intemperie.

TONGUE,
Designed by Ross Didier
Made by ROSS DIDIER
www.rossdidier.com

Indoor and outdoor chaise lounge hand made limited edition of ten.
" I simply wanted to build a very, very sexy piece ... from all angles ! "
The moulded fibreglass form is coated in sprayed polyurethane rubber being a surface toughening technique that Australian utility vans "Utes" use for the back of their open trays for work and surfing.

Materials: fibreglass , polyurethane rubber.
Size: 185x120x60 cm.

El diseñador Ross Didier nos presenta esta sexy chaise lounge realizada completamente a mano en una edición limitada de diez.
"¡Simplemente quería construir una pieza muy, muy sexy...desde todos los ángulos!"
La fibra de vidrio una vez moldeada se rocía con el caucho de poliuretano en espray, esta es una técnica utilizada en Australia para endurecer las furgonetas de transporte "Utes" y también las tablas de surf.

Materiales: fibra de vidrio y caucho de poliuretano.
Dimensiones: 185x120x60 cm

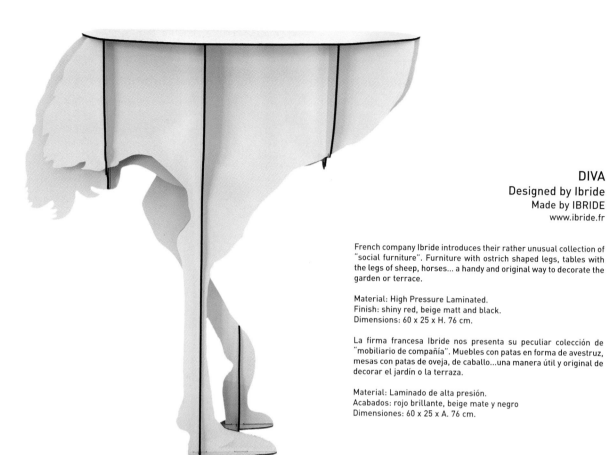

DIVA
Designed by Ibride
Made by IBRIDE
www.ibride.fr

French company Ibride introduces their rather unusual collection of "social furniture". Furniture with ostrich shaped legs, tables with the legs of sheep, horses... a handy and original way to decorate the garden or terrace.

Material: High Pressure Laminated.
Finish: shiny red, beige matt and black.
Dimensions: 60 x 25 x H. 76 cm.

La firma francesa Ibride nos presenta su peculiar colección de "mobiliario de compañía". Muebles con patas en forma de avestruz, mesas con patas de oveja, de caballo...una manera útil y original de decorar el jardín o la terraza.

Material: Laminado de alta presión.
Acabados: rojo brillante, beige mate y negro
Dimensiones: 60 x 25 x A. 76 cm.

XXL
Designed by Kettal
Made by KETTAL
www.kettalgroup.com

From Kettal comes a new collection of designer furniture for the terrace. Both the sofas and chairs and the rest of this modular collection are traditionally hand woven. The tubular aluminium structure is covered in a high quality synthetic fibre which like the frame is highly resistant to the elements.

Kettal nos presenta su nueva colección de muebles de diseño para terraza. Tanto los sofás como las sillas y el resto de la colección modular se presentan con un trenzado a mano artesanalmente. La structura en tubo de aluminio recubierto con fibra sintética de gran calidad y resistencia como su chasis, resistente a la intemperie.

VITEO
Designed by Viteo
Made by VITEO
www.viteo.at

From Viteo, a new collection of outdoor furniture. Tables which transform into improvised bench seats or sun-loungers which can be transformed into tables according to preference. Made from wood which is resistant to both high and low temperatures, this modular system invites us to relax in our spare time.

Viteo nos presenta su nueva colección de muebles de exterior. Mesas que se transforman en inprovisados bancos, o tumbonas que se transforman en improvisadas mesas según nos interese. Realizada en madera resistente a altas y bajas temperaturas, esta sistema modular nos invita al relax en nuestro tiempo libre.